HENRY HATFIELD is Professor of German Literature at Harvard University, where he has taught since 1954. He has received Guggenheim and Fulbright fellowships and was Visiting Professor at the Free University of Berlin. He was general editor of the *Germanic Review* from 1947 to 1953 and has served on both the editorial board and the executive committee of the Modern Language Association. Professor Hatfield is the author of numerous books and articles; his most recent books are *Goethe: A Critical Introduction, Aesthetic Paganism in German Literature,* and *Modern German Literature.*

CRISIS AND CONTINUITY IN MODERN GERMAN FICTION *Ten Essays*

CRISIS AND CONTINUITY IN MODERN GERMAN FICTION *Ten Essays*

by Henry Hatfield

Cornell University Press • ITHACA AND LONDON

First published 1969

Standard Book Number 8014-0523-8

Library of Congress Catalog Card Number 70-87019

PRINTED IN THE UNITED STATES OF AMERICA
BY VAIL-BALLOU PRESS, INC.

For Walter Grossmann,
Margaret Guenther,
and Frank Ryder

PREFACE

In this book I discuss representative works of nine German and Austrian writers, recent or contemporary, who seem particularly interesting to me. I do not claim that my selection includes all of the most important authors; some readers may find one or two of the choices questionable. Few students of the subject, it seems clear, will object to the inclusion of Fontane, Thomas Mann, Kafka, Hesse, Musil, and Broch; the others may be more debatable. A very good case could be made for including Heinrich Mann, Alfred Döblin, and possibly Franz Werfel. Arthur Schnitzler, a master of short forms, wrote only one novel; Arnold Zweig never again attained the heights of *The Case of Sergeant Grischa.*

I have not attempted to give a historical account of German fiction. (In this book "German" literature refers to the language used, not the political provenience.) For one thing, this would have meant the exclusion of the novels of Günter Grass and Uwe Johnson, since the critic, although he ought to be able to respond usefully to any challenging book, however recent, cannot see it in perspective until some time has passed. He can sensibly argue that *Doctor Faustus* or *The Tin Drum* is an important book but can hardly determine its position among twentieth-century novels.

For practical reasons I have discussed a short story by Franz Kafka rather than a novel: first, because Kafka's works are so complex that they demand explication paragraph by paragraph and often line by line; second, since none of his novels was finished, only the short narratives are complete aesthetic units.

The books discussed are treated in roughly chronological order, with one major exception: the chapter on *Doctor Faustus* is placed last—not because it is the most technical of these essays (though it is), but because *Doctor Faustus* seems to me a sort of end point, the *ne plus ultra* of a special kind of novel.

After finishing this book, I found that the works of Thomas Mann figure in it repeatedly as points of reference, and sometimes as norms, though never, I hope, as Procrustean standards. This focus on Mann was not my conscious intention, but to the extent that it helps give the book cohesion, it may be justifiable.

It is my pleasant duty to thank Theodore Ziolkowski for his helpful criticism of the entire manuscript, and Bernhard Boeschenstein, Joachim Bumke, Ritta-Jo Horsley, Walther Killy, Katharina and Momme Mommsen, Cynthia Peters, Albrecht Schoene, Sandra Shuman, John Spiegel, J. M. Stein, and A. Leslie Willson for their comments on individual chapters, as well as my Harvard class on modern German fiction for helpful criticism. I am grateful to Peter Wapnewski and other colleagues at the Free University of Berlin for providing me with pleasant working quarters, to the library staff at the Free University, and to Hans Wysling and Marianne Fischer of the Thomas Mann Archive in Zurich. Above all I wish to thank my wife for numerous suggestions and for typing the whole work with cheerful patience.

For permission to incorporate material from several of my articles I am grateful to the editors and publishers: to Vandenhoeck & Ruprecht, from "Myth versus Secularism," in *Festschrift für Bernhard Blume*, edited by Egon Schwarz, Hunter G. Hannum, and Edgar Lohner (Göttingen, 1967), pages 271–279; to the University of Texas Press, from "Günter Grass: The Artist as Satirist," in *The Contemporary Novel in German: A Symposium*, edited by Robert R. Heitner (Austin, 1967), pages 117–134; to *Books Abroad* (Summer, 1967), from "The Human Tragicomedy: Doderer's *Die Wasserfalle von Slunj*"; to the copyright owners, the Regents of the University of Wisconsin, from "Vitality and Tradition: Heimito von Doderer's *Die Strudlhofstiege*," *Monatshefte*, Volume XLVII, Number 1 (1955), the University of Wisconsin Press; and to the editors of *Euphorion*, Volume LXII, Number 4 (1968), for "The Magic Square: Thomas Mann's *Doktor Faustus*." The last three articles appeared in a form somewhat different from that in this book.

HENRY HATFIELD

Cambridge, Massachusetts
February 1969

CONTENTS

INTRODUCTION

All the authors discussed in this book have in common a sense of crisis. Because all of them, with one exception, experienced one or both of the world wars and other catastrophes, this anxious awareness may seem all too natural; but there are less obvious reasons for it. Since Nietzsche, premonitions of a cataclysmic shift in the course of history and perhaps in the direction of man's development have formed part of the intellectual climate of Central Europe. Even the first of the novelists considered here, Theodor Fontane, who lived in a relatively stable society and witnessed Bismarck's triumphs and the founding and growth of the German Empire, divined that startling changes were imminent. His *Effi Briest* implies the decadence of the old order; *Der Stechlin,* his last novel, indicates that revolutionary upheavals are inevitable.

Of course the feeling that man is on the verge or in the midst of an ordeal, fraught with danger but perhaps also with promise, varies in intensity with different authors. In Franz Kafka's "A Country Doctor" the mood is the blackest: the ice age has already set in. It has similarly begun in the last volume of Hermann Broch's *The Sleepwalkers,* but the author conveys the countervailing hope that the time must "dialectically" shift to a radically different era. "If winter comes, . . ." Hermann Hesse's *Steppenwolf* views ever recurring and painful crises as basic to the normal development of the genuine human being—and presumably of society itself. The most excruciating turning points may be the most fruitful. At the end of *Dog Years,* Günter Grass presents his fellow citizens as a host of programmed automata; his reaction is the indignation of the true satirist, not despair.

Fortunately, not even the writers most obsessed with crisis devote all their books to it; comedy and epic have their places, along with tragedy. Thomas Mann's *Doctor Faustus* is the most shattering of the depictions of cultural revolution, but his *Joseph and His Brothers* is a serene, often comic book. Before presenting "the Cannae of Austrian freedom" in *The Demons,* Heimito von Doderer showed the generally benign aspects of Viennese life in *Die Strudlhofstiege* ("The Strudlhof Stairway"). The sense of danger is often balanced by the belief that man is a tough creature who tends to persist, if only by the narrowest of margins. Similarly, while the crisis—and even the death—of the novel have been often announced in the last twenty years, the form persists.

In the last analysis, crisis and continuity complement each other. As Fontane implies in *Der Stechlin,* true continuity includes revolutionary periods without which life and history would be stagnant. Robert Musil's Törless is helped more than harmed by the pangs and humiliations of his adolescence; Uwe Johnson's heroine D. surmounts political and personal dangers and sets out quietly to construct a new existence to replace the one she has had to abandon. Even in *Doctor Faustus* the final note is that of "hope beyond hopelessness"; Leverkühn's music, and presumably even his guilty nation, will survive.

Long treated condescendingly by critics, the novel is especially attractive as a form today because it is flexible enough to adapt itself to almost any situation. I am not thinking primarily of sheer length; Musil's *Young Törless* contains much more in its 130 pages than do most long novels. Yet the novelist must have space enough and time to present a broad panorama if he so desires, to extend his scope horizontally. Broch's *The Sleepwalkers* and Grass's *The Tin Drum* and *Dog Years* are relevant here. Novels about whole cities—Paris, Berlin, Dublin—can hardly be brief. If on the other hand the novelist wishes to analyze an individual, he needs, as it were, vertical scope—whether he traces his hero's development in a *Bildungsroman*, employs Freudian or Jungian insights like Broch or Hesse, or presents him in terms of myth, as Mann does with Jacob in *Joseph*. It is equally possible to make us thoroughly acquainted with a person by presenting him or her in a series of dramatic scenes, as Fontane shows us Effi Briest. Little by little, with minimal intrusion by the narrator, the various facets of her character appear.

Although no historical account is attempted in these essays, it may be helpful to indicate where each of the writers discussed fits in chronologically. Writers of several generations appear. Fontane, the great-grandfather of the contemporary German novel, was born in 1819, but his finest works did not appear until the late eighties and the nineties. Mann and Hesse were born in the 1870's; Musil, Kafka, and Broch in the following decade; Doderer in the nineties. Grass and Johnson were born in 1927 and 1934 respectively, more than a century after Fontane. These writers reflect a variety of literary movements, from late-nineteenth-century realism to the *nouveau roman*. They have not been chosen, however, as illustrations of any mode or ism. Great artists transcend such classifications; it would be futile to try to label Musil, Kafka, or Mann, for example.

Each essay tries to show, implicitly or explicitly, why

the particular book or author merits our attention; it may, however, be helpful to indicate very briefly here the special qualities and contributions of the various writers. Fontane, in his unpretentious way, guided the novel away from metaphysics toward a concern with society, from romanticism toward realism. Along with various non-German writers—especially Tolstoy, Dostoevsky, Flaubert, and Zola—he laid the foundations of the modern German novel.

Fontane reasserted a European as against a parochial note in the novel; Mann did much to make German fiction known throughout Europe and beyond. In part he may be seen as a renovator of old subgenres, like the family novel and the *Bildungsroman;* in part he parodied them. Similarly, his mythical novel *Joseph* is both serious and ironic. Hesse is perhaps the last of the romantics. Much of his earlier work is so much in the tradition of the German "lyrical novel" that its international appeal is limited. One suspects also that books like *The Journey to the East* and *Siddhartha* are widely read today mainly because their insights into Oriental wisdom are particularly attractive to mystically minded youths. Technically brilliant, far less adolescent in tone and mood than is much of Hesse's work, *Der Steppenwolf* develops his favorite themes with aesthetic distance and humor.

Although the old Austro-Hungarian Empire was marked by conservatism in literature as well as in politics, it was the birthplace of the three boldest experimenters among the writers discussed here—Kafka, Musil, and Broch. Aside from their radical originality, the three do not seem to have a great deal in common. The Austrian "national characteristics" are supposed to include devotion to tradition, wit, sophistication, and skepticism. All three authors are, to be sure, concerned with tradition: they imply, from quite separate points of view, that the major traditions underlying contemporary society are dying or dead. Both Kafka and Musil are indeed skeptical, but in radically different ways. Painfully diffident about his own genius, Kafka characteristically wrote parables or fables about the human condition. He treated, in a style of great purity and economy, a single theme again and again: the virtual impossibility of acquiring true knowledge, and hence of achieving salvation or even communication. Compared to Kafka, Musil and Broch seem downright optimistic. Musil aimed to provide, in *The Man without Qualities*, not only a panorama of Austrian (and by inference European) society in decline, but a reconciliation of the two spheres of "precision" and "soul," to combine the scientific and the nonrational aspects of life in a solution which he himself called Utopian. It is hardly surprising that *The Man without Qualities* was never finished. Even more ambitious than Musil, Broch hoped to write "epistemological novels" providing a total picture of society *and* a solution of man's problems. He was obsessed by the utter decadence of the contemporary world and by the hope of overcoming it dialectically. Since he believed that literature could show "man in his wholeness" and contribute to his purification, he was convinced that the novelist should play a lofty moral role. Broch is a sort of Faust or Captain Ahab among novelists, out to conquer the absolute—and thus anything but "Austrian" in the usual sense.

In contrast, Doderer is very Austrian indeed. His novels are saturated with Viennese tradition, wit, and a certain very reputable type of conservatism. It seems right to include him, not only because he is, at his best, a very gifted novelist, but to indicate that strands of convention as well as of revolt form part of the fabric of any literature. To be sure, Doderer hoped like Broch to present a total image of life in his novels, but his techniques are not those of an innovator.

As has been noted, it is too early to state with any precision the literary locus of writers as close to us as are Grass and Johnson. Grass is a writer of great versatility, a master of language who recalls Rabelais and Joyce. His great danger is excess: sometimes the feast is too lavish, the devices are too ingenious, the books too long. When he stays within the more disciplined form of the novella, he avoids the danger: *Cat and Mouse* is his finest work. Johnson is more limited in scope and theme, and perhaps the purer artist. His main concern—the difficulty of attaining truth—reminds one of Kafka, but Johnson approaches it in a highly original way. All his books are set in the divided Germany of the present, in which citizens of the two half-nations find it increasingly difficult to understand each other's language. In his earlier novels, this difficulty is so well presented that the reader himself often does not quite know what is going on, but Johnson's third published novel, *Two Views*, shows that he has solved this problem.

CRISIS AND CONTINUITY IN MODERN GERMAN FICTION *Ten Essays*

1/ The Renovation of the German Novel: Theodor Fontane

"There are no indisputable truths; and if there are any, they're boring."

"I have always had a highly developed sense for *facts*. I have always taken life as I found it and submitted myself to it. That is, externally—not in my mind."

—Theodor Fontane

Coming as they did after the age of Goethe, the German writers of the nineteenth century faced the handicaps of anyone following after greatness. Inevitably, if unfairly, we tend to judge them, as they often judged themselves, by their predecessors. While they achieved triumphs in the lyric and considerable success in the drama and the novella, they were much less happy in the novel. Indeed, their attainment in that genre may be described as, on the whole, dull but improving. To be sure, several talented writers emerged—figures like Stifter, Keller, and Raabe, who are still valued and read today—but their presence is hardly felt beyond the frontiers of the German language. Others, like Gutzkow, Freytag, and Spielhagen, who once enjoyed high prestige, are regarded today primarily as figures of historical importance or at the most as contributors to literary theory; their works are no longer really alive. Social and political reasons have been suggested for this state of affairs, including censorship and the lack of a great literary capital like Paris or London—though Tolstoy and Dostoevsky overcame handicaps severer than those existing in Central Europe.

Further, the drift of German literature toward "inwardness," at least since the days of romanticism and philosophical idealism, was strong enough largely to counteract the realistic currents of the age. (Of course there were exceptions, but these were often resented like Heine, or ignored like Georg Büchner, or deficient in talent like Gutzkow and Spielhagen.) To many German writers of the time, nature was more interesting than society, the small town or country estate than the city, the introverted if gifted eccentric than a man living in a viable community. In fact, society and the city were often seen as evil or at least dangerous in themselves; one should flee "the world" and the metropolis, as authors from Eichendorff to Stifter suggested. Since it seems broadly true that the novel is by nature primarily a realistic and so to speak an extroverted genre, the relative weakness of German fiction in the nineteenth century is not surprising. (No one would deny that great unrealistic and antirealistic novels exist; I am speaking of the main thrust of the form.) If the German novel of the century seems provincial and old-fashioned, unexciting compared to the English, French, Russian, and even the American achievement, its lack of convincingly realistic qualities is at least one major cause of its relative mediocrity. Several representative writers—one thinks of Storm, Keller, and Otto Ludwig—combined realistic detail with a nonrealistic, often didactic intention; this compromise has been labeled "poetic realism." Often there is a lyric strain, a reminiscence of the fairy tale, in their stories. Lichtenberg observed a century earlier that the Germans needed a common-sense genius like Fielding rather than another inspired bard like Klopstock. Certainly a genuine realist was more urgently required than another Hölderlin or Mörike.

The works, especially the later novels, of Theodor Fontane provide the one great exception in a rather dreary literary picture. This is increasingly recognized: an edition of his complete works has recently appeared,[1] as have important books by Peter Demetz[2] and Richard Brinkmann;[3] there is a spate of essays, articles, and dissertations. In itself all this activity would prove little: literary rehabilitations are so frequent that one often has the feeling that this or that "unjustly neglected" author is being resuscitated *faute de mieux*. The increased interest in Fontane—not "revival," for he was never forgotten—is based on valid grounds. He is an important—not a dominating—figure in world literature, and he had a stimulating and liberating impact on the later development of the novel in German. One of the most modest of writers, Fontane had no notion that he might exert such an influence. He did so, however, as the novels of Eduard von Keyserling, Thomas Mann (especially his *Buddenbrooks*), and the first section of Broch's *The Sleepwalkers* attest. He was not only excellent himself but a cause of excellence in other men. To demonstrate this point, which has not yet been sufficiently emphasized outside of Germany, is the aim of this essay. I hope to indicate Fontane's contributions as the cofounder of the modern German novel, with special attention to three of his representative books; *Frau Jenny Treibel*, *Effi Briest*, and *Der Stechlin*.[4] Each of them differs greatly from the others, but each has an unmistakably Fontanean tone.

By his background and by his early experiences, Fontane was admirably equipped to play the part of a close but critical observer of the Prussian scene. His Huguenot ancestry is often adduced, in praise or in blame, as a cause of the

"French," unsentimental character of his work. If this is meant racially, it is nonsense, but Fontane's acquaintance and sympathy with French culture may have been an important shaping factor; and as a man whose family came from abroad, he was very much aware that Germany was only one among several important nations.

In his youth Fontane spent several impressionable years in Swinemünde, a seaport on the Baltic where he came into contact with people of many nations. Until he was thirty, he had to support himself as an apothecary in provincial towns and in Berlin. He started to write even then, and was fortunate to be made a member, despite his rather humble status, of the Berlin literary club The Tunnel over the Spree. After turning to journalism, he made three stays in London, one of them very protracted, supporting himself as a correspondent of various Prussian newspapers. His strong though not uncritical interest in English literature, history, and traditions left its mark on his own work. He was indebted to the English novel from Scott through Dickens and was enthusiastic about border ballads. Later he wrote successful ballads of his own. Typically, "Archibald Douglas," the most famous of these, has a Scottish, not a German, theme; but he did not neglect the native scene, as his five volumes devoted to the Prussian countryside (*Wanderungen durch die Mark Brandenburg*) show. During Bismarck's three wars (1864, 1866, 1870–1871) Fontane served as a correspondent with the army. Thus like Mark Twain, Hemingway, and others, he learned his literary trade largely during an apprenticeship as a practicing journalist. If his formal education was slight, his training as a writer was admirable. He was diffident about his talent and remained so even after his finest works had appeared.

In fact, he is a classical example of the literary "late bloomer"; his first novel, *Vor dem Sturm* ("Before the Storm"), was published in 1878, when he was fifty-nine; his great period did not begin until he was almost seventy. It is no accident that wise, ironic old men appear frequently in his later books.

Even more frequent are "foreign" figures—English, French, Jewish, American, and others. They are generally more interesting than his German characters, and often more attractive. Fontane normally presents his persons with a mixture of sympathy and irony; the former generally prevails in his treatment of "outsiders," whether foreigners or native eccentrics. Although it may well be true that the society in which he moved was class-conscious rather than race-conscious,[5] he was keenly aware of various prejudices, especially anti-Semitism. He wrote to his friend Georg Friedlaender that he would be much more annoyed with the Jews if the Christians were not far worse than they.[6]

Although he was anything but a snob, Fontane had a very acute sense of class distinctions. The Prussian aristocracy—young officers, ambitious civil servants, and rural Junkers—play a dominant part in his stories, but he refused to idealize the nobles or any other class. Thus his very sympathetic depiction of an affair between a lieutenant and a lower-class Berlin girl, in *Irrungen, Wirrungen* (*Trials and Tribulations*), was resented by conservative critics.[7] Although he felt that the abolition of the aristocracy would "remove the last remainder of poetry from the world," [8] he also wrote, "The country gentry, though I am particularly devoted to them, no longer fit into the modern world." [9] As J. P. Stern wittily said about Fontane's politics, "'Two cheers for aristocracy' could well be *his* motto." [10] His attitude toward the nobility is complicated but hardly ambivalent.

The one class Fontane rejected was the bourgeoisie, and even here he excepted the bourgeois of genius, the grand-scale entrepreneur.[11] Otherwise, his attitude is consistently negative; he once used the uncharacteristic expression "bourgeois worm." [12] In his depiction of the rich middle class, especially in *Frau Jenny Treibel*, he at times crosses the frontier separating irony from satire; yet the individual bourgeois, including the ineffable Frau Jenny, is never treated with the harshness of a Flaubert. As Brinkmann shows, Fontane can be an implacable critic in his letters but tends toward a conciliatory attitude in his books.[13] The former are not more "sincere" than the latter; the narrator of a novel has concerns different from the letter writer's.

Fontane was so concerned with the threat embodied by the bourgeois element—the cult of money and possessions—that he felt that even the Social Democrats had been infected by it.[14] Although the proletarians in his novels play only minor roles, he was convinced in old age that the future would begin with the fourth estate; "the others may just as well lie down and die." [15] His last project, never carried out, was a novel about a picturesque group of late-medieval communists, the *Likedeeler* ("Equal Sharers"). One should not conclude that Fontane was "on the way to Marx"—he remained very much the individualist—but his openness to change, in politics and elsewhere, is beyond question and become more pronounced in old age. Or, as Thomas Mann put it, after seventy Fontane became younger every year.[16]

Fontane believed in no philosophical or theological system. Thoroughly antimetaphysical, "de-Hegelized," he remained very much the pragmatist who "always submitted to life as [he] found it." [17] (He did not make an idol of "adjustment" and was never uncritical, but his books, like his letters, convey the frequent necessity of resignation.) Brinkmann well speaks of Fontane's "realistic situation ethics"; [18] there are few absolutes. Thus adultery may well lead to disaster but may be preferable to the prolongation of a dead marriage; dueling is a brutal, fundamentally stupid institution but one which certain people in certain situations must uphold; and so on. Fontane's own implicit code seems based largely on a secularized Christianity but modified by his concepts of the English gentleman and the Prussian officer of the old school. It is characteristic that some of his most attractive persons are nondogmatic Christians, like Pastor Lorenzen and Dubslav von Stechlin in *Der Stechlin*, whereas the orthodox canoness and the overambitious churchman in the same novel are almost repulsive. Despite his regard for Christianity, Fontane maintained, very typically, that the nature of its religious challenge was excessively radical: "The dubious thing about Christianity is that it makes demands which no human can fulfill—and if someone does fulfill them, one becomes more anxious and worried than ever. One has to shudder at a victory which had better never been won." [19] It is the old protest of the humanist against the "holy barbarian"; Fontane is of the tribe of Montaigne and Erasmus.

Fontane's independence of party and dogma is complemented by his keenness of insight. "I don't see things black; I only see," he wrote Friedlaender.[20] Although there are some very effective impressionistic scenes in his novels, particularly evocations of country inns, lakes, and rivers in Prussia, Fontane was much more interested in man than in nature. Social and political matters, however important, are subordinated to individuals: he did not write *romans à thèse*. Nor did he accept the nineteenth-century belief in the determining influence of milieu: "Life has taught me that everything depends on human beings, not on so-called conditions [*Verhältnisse*]." [21] He remained profoundly the rationalist in a culture which has generally underrated its brilliant rationalists, from Wieland and Lichtenberg on. Fontane preserved his clear-sighted independence toward the idols of the time. He regarded Bismarck with mingled admiration and misgivings, and viewed "culture heroes" with equal skepticism: Dubslav von Stechlin is properly devastating about Nietzsche's idea of the superman; the favorite composers of the *nouveau riche* Jenny Treibel are Meyerbeer and Wagner.

Perhaps there may be a connection between Fontane's rationalism and his avoidance of emotional intensity in his fiction. More likely his shying away from passion has something to do with his age at the time he wrote his novels: an author is not likely to produce *The Sorrows of Young Werther* or *Lady Chatterley's Lover* at seventy, however fresh and lively his mind may be. This cool emotional tone seems to derive from Fontane's characteristic tendency toward understatement. Like Lessing's Nathan, he liked to observe calmly but was by no means unfeeling.

Fontane's tendency to shun emotional scenes accounts for one of the clear limitations of his talent: with one very "real" area of life, the sexual, he did not care, or dare, to deal. Perhaps we may speak of another "refusal to be great"; [22] but if it was a refusal it was an unconscious one —Fontane, to the best of my knowledge, never thought of himself under the category of potential greatness. Within the limits of what time, place, and his own taste permitted, Fontane's fidelity to telling the truth is unquestionable.

Realism as he understood it, excluded four elements: lying, forced effects, cloudy vagueness, and the obsolete (*das Abgestorbene*).[23] Sometimes he admittedly used rather trashy devices (*Mumpitz*) to make his books effective;[24] if the devices worked, he accepted them, however ruefully. Occasionally he lapsed into sentimentality: the last section of *Effi Briest,* otherwise probably his best novel, is disturbingly "sweet." Such aberrations are rare in Fontane, very rare in his last novels.

In the main, Fontane achieves his "nonpoetic" realism in three ways. First, he keeps his focus almost always on human beings in society. The letters and diaries his characters write are concerned with relations between people rather than with an isolated ego. Even when Effi Briest has been banished from "society," it is the pressures from those who have cast her out and the pull toward those she may not see which shape her life. Second, praise and blame are distributed in a way which is actually very lifelike. Effi, her lover Crampas, her husband, and her parents, who are after all responsible for her education and for encouraging her in her hasty decision to marry, are all culpable for her "fall," yet we have little sense of moral guilt—except in Crampas' case—or even of a single tragically irrevocable misstep. (This effect is partly due to Fontane's discreet "veiling" technique.) Such ironic balancing is equally observable in Fontane's comic novel *Frau Jenny Treibel:* almost everyone in the book, not only the newly rich Treibels, is more or less ridiculous and needs some sort of mild lesson in behavior. Third, as Brinkmann very acutely points out, Fontane gains credibility and a large degree of objectivity by a dialectic stratagem.[25] As the subjectivity of his various narrators becomes clear, the intelligent reader allows for it, consciously or unconsciously. Thus the narrator of *Effi Briest* is obviously very partial to the heroine; of *Der Stechlin,* to the hero. Only on second thought does the reader perceive that Dubslav von Stechlin is often not as liberal as the general impression, the "image" he projects in the novel, has led him to expect.

Georg Lukács has presented a darker picture of Fontane in a cogently argued, by no means unsympathetic essay.[26] Lukács contends that Fontane's delayed development was partly caused by conditions in Prussia and his own poverty. Although he had been an enthusiastic supporter of the revolution of 1848, he was forced for economic reasons to write for conservative journals, including the ultrareactionary *Kreuzzeitung*. Lukács concedes that the novelist never became a mercenary scribbler but argues persuasively that Fontane preserved his personal integrity only by keeping the public and the private sphere apart from each other, of course a dangerous expedient. As the deficiencies of Bismarck's new empire became more apparent, the critic maintains, Fontane's awareness of them enabled him to become a far better and a more realistic writer. Yet he remained skeptical about the possibilities of social action and suffered from moods of nihilism. Thus the "misery," as Marx put it, of German conditions inhibited his full literary growth. There is, I think, much truth in this analysis. When Lukács maintains, however, that Fontane could have found the answer to all his problems by going to the nearest bookstore and buying the works of Marx and Engels, one remains unconvinced, to put it mildly.

To turn to specific contributions: Fontane first raised the German *Zeitroman*, the fictional picture of an age, to a work of art.[27] (Various writers—Gutzkow, Spielhagen, and Freytag most prominently—had attempted "time novels" around mid-century, but their intentions are more interesting than their books.) Similarly, while novelists since Grimmelshausen had introduced large cities in their books —Keller's evocation of nineteenth-century Munich is very colorful—one can say that Fontane's Berlin is the first important city to play a convincing and central role in the German novel.

Fontane's famous conversations often form the most strikingly successful sections of his novels. Typically they take place before, during, or after a dinner party or in the course of a *Landpartie*[28] (an excursion to the country, normally combining a walk or ride through pleasant scenery with the national sport: group eating and drinking). Like churchgoing in the bourgeois drama, the *Landpartie* further offered the nineteenth-century writer a chance to bring his hero and heroine together with little or no chaperonage. Fontane's people generally talk in a lively, amusing, mildly witty way—sometimes of course a figure is involuntarily amusing. One does not find in them the wit of an Oscar Wilde or of an Arthur Schnitzler; rather, at their most representative, they produce pleasant, relaxed chat—*Plauderei.* The topic of conversation hardly matters, but at times the subject chosen betrays a great deal about national standards of taste. At a dinner, Lieutenant von Czako, presumably a person of discrimination, regales his partner with an account of rat-catching in the sewers of Paris.[29] But if the quality of Fontane's dialogue is at times less than sparkling, it must be said that he manages the talk very effectively to show us two or more points of view almost simultaneously or to reveal much in a few unimportant-seeming remarks.[30] In some instances, when a crucial action is signaled, we do not understand the course of events until later. This is the case during the weeks when Effi Briest is being increasingly fascinated by Major Crampas. At the end of an important scene in *Der Stechlin,* Armgard von Barby tells her surprised sister, "I almost think I'm engaged," and the reader, startled, quickly retraces his steps. Occasionally one learns more from a character's silences than from his words.[31]

Peter Demetz has shown that several of Fontane's novels tend toward dramatic organization, much as Jane Austen's do.[32] In fact *Effi Briest* partially fulfills Percy Lubbock's criteria for the dramatic novel.[33] The novel is essentially a series of dramatic pictures; two of these scenes, both very important, could be staged without changing the dialogue —Innstetten's fatal conversation with a friend about dueling, and the confrontation between the divorced Effi and her daughter.

Just as the term "situation ethics" has been used to characterize Fontane's moral evaluations, one could speak of his "situation style." In other words, he consciously adjusts his manner to his theme. A real writer, he maintains, derives "his continually varied style from the subject he is treating."[34] Fontane largely fulfilled this aim of suiting the style to the matter at hand. *Effi Briest*, an admirably constructed, symmetrically shaped novel, is written with great economy of means. In *Der Stechlin,* where there is an "additive"[35] accumulation of incidents rather than a really focused plot, the style is deliberately casual and almost verbose. In a famous critique of Gottfried Keller, Fontane remarked that the old definition of style as the flavor of the individual writer—"le style c'est l'homme"—was out of date. Rather, "the more objective a work is, the more style it has."[36] By "objectivity" he meant here freedom from those characteristics of an author which are not appropriate to the subject he presents. In this sense Keller, whose strong personality marked every page he wrote, indeed lacked style.

It was pointed out long ago, correctly, that from this point of view Fontane's own prose would be vulnerable.[37] His figures, especially in *Der Stechlin,* tend to speak in his own unique, chatty, and often witty way. The officers von Rex and von Czako in *Der Stechlin* converse more delightfully than actual Prussian lieutenants presumably did.[38] Like Lessing, another master of dialogue, he often had even his rather dull characters speak with real verve. In *Der Stechlin,* Fontane goes very far in this direction, but one can hardly regret this literary license. Good conversation is a rarer achievement than the accurate recording of mediocre talk. Precisely because of his charm of style, Fontane felt free, in his last years, from having to tell a story in the conventional sense. He wrote of his late story *Die Poggenpuhls* ("The Poggenpuhl Sisters"): "The book is no novel and has no contents. 'How' has to take the place of 'What' —there's nothing I like better." [39]

On balance, Fontane appears as the one German novelist of his century whose work has not significantly aged, whose best books still seem "modern" in a laudatory sense. This being so, one wonders why he is so little known internationally. There seem to be two main reasons. First, Berlin has never had the "romantic" aura of Paris, London, or Rome. After 1914, the association "Berlin—Prussia—Junker—William II—war" was a chilling one; Nazism, though hardly of Prussian origin, made the situation even worse. An English or American publisher could hardly be blamed for hesitating to bring out novels set in that milieu. On a literary level, it could be objected that Jane Austen and Turgenev, comparably gifted and vastly better known, "got there first"—well ahead of Fontane.

The advocate of Fontane can answer both of these objections, at least partially. Although, like Kipling, he had a weakness for the military, his books are anything but glorifications of the Hohenzollern establishment. He belongs primarily to the liberal Berlin tradition, extending from Lessing and Moses Mendelssohn to the present. And granted that Jane Austen got there first (and is even more readable) it is hardly sensible to neglect any writer of that general order of excellence. Fontane is too good to waste.

Frau Jenny Treibel

One of Fontane's most successful works, *Frau Jenny Treibel* (1893), is a comedy in the form of a novel. Although the superficially sentimental protagonist, as hypocritical as she is greedy, could equally well have been made the object of a satire, the satiric mode did not really appeal to the author. (Some twenty years later, Carl Sternheim made comparable figures the centers of his fiercely amusing comedies.) Potentially a horrible creature, Jenny does relatively little harm, and the comedy ends, very traditionally, with one marriage and the prospect of another. Not even the most passionately metaphysical German critic could find anything "deep" in this story.

Actually, the book could easily be adapted to the stage. One group of scenes takes place at the house of Professor Wilibald Schmidt, a pleasant old fellow with a touch of Fontanean irony. His attractive daughter Corinna, weary of living on a modest academic scale, would like to marry money—which brings us to the Treibels, at whose mansion most of the other action ensues. Jenny Treibel, nee Bürstenbinder, once the professor's sweetheart, jilted him years before to escape from extremely humble circumstances, but the two have remained friends. An extremely clever girl, Corinna maneuvers Jenny's weak if well-meaning son Leopold into proposing; Jenny intervenes firmly and successfully. Before long Corinna realizes her error. Embarrassed but by no means heartbroken, she accepts a suitor of her own class; Leopold will also marry within his own financial stratum. Jenny is one of the guests at Corinna's wedding. As Peter Demetz remarks, *Frau Jenny Treibel* is constructed with "sovereign artistry." [40] The action alternates between the Treibels' and the Schmidts' domains; Corinna's three crucial encounters with the Treibels occur at well-calculated intervals.

The book is appropriately rich in comic devices. Fontane inclined to use significant names, often with humorous overtones.[41] The combination Corinna Schmidt, uniting the classical with the all too ordinary, suggests the mixed quality of life in a professor's household. (Helene Ölhafen, in Mann's *Doctor Faustus*, like her husband, Serenus Zeitblom, was apparently named with a similar suggestion in mind.) A grotesque supporter of the rich Herr Treibel is called Vogelsang; another hanger-on of the family, a tenor past his prime, is Adolar Krola. Even the young man who eventually marries Corinna has been christened Marcell Widderkopp; his last name suggests stubbornness. When Fontane labels two of Schmidt's friends Kuh and Rindfleisch, he seems to be overdoing things. A few names either suggest social class, like Schmidt, or furnish local color, like Schmolke.

The Treibels' circle of friends, like Professor Schmidt's, contains a large proportion of eccentrics, some harmlessly amusing, a few grotesque like Lieutenant Vogelsang. It is characteristic of Fontane that he made this sworn foe of the nobility the most ridiculous figure in the book. Fontane's use of slight occurrences to anticipate larger ones is very adroit: Jenny Treibel, in an expansive, "idealistic" mood, actually suggests to Corinna that her son might well marry a professor's daughter; later, Leopold's inability to overrule his mother when forbidden a second cup of coffee points ahead to his failure as Corinna's fiancé.

The flaws of the various characters are comic rather than tragic. Given her background, it is understandable that Corinna wants to marry for money. She is honest about her own motives throughout—as most of Fontane's persons are. Herr Treibel's ambitions for rank and title lead him to make a fool of himself in politics, but he too takes humiliation gracefully. When the amiable pedagogue Schmidt gets tipsy at his daughter's wedding, he merely adds a mildly Aristophanic note at the comedy's end.

Only Jenny's defects are serious ones; here the reader sense that he is dealing with potential viciousness and that the book is no longer merely an entertainment. She is the only "round" character in the book—though as Edwin Muir writes, there is nothing wrong with "flat" characters as such.[42] Jenny is not without a few redeeming qualities. She is very astute and she is capable of real, though never disinterested, honesty when affairs become critical. If she were merely a fool, like Frau Stöhr in *The Magic Mountain,* she would not be dangerous. While her cultural pretensions are a sham, she does not make gross blunders, betraying herself only by her parroting of clichés and modish "in words" and occasionally by embarrassing metaphors, as when she says, to explain a poor night's sleep, "That dreadful Vogelsang lay on me like a nightmare all night." She is devoted to sentimental music and poetry and is not consciously insincere when she claims she despises money. When the threat of her son's marrying Corinna arises, it shocks her out of her seeming schizophrenia: she tells him that there is no real happiness without "the foundations which support life"—meaning money in quantity. She is clever enough to point out to Corinna, quite correctly, that the girl does not really love Leopold. Here one might ask, What if she had? But of course we are in the world of comedy. Fontane leans over backward to take Jenny lightly: when she feigns a faint—of course as a stratagem—he notes that "like most unconscious women, she wasn't unconscious enough not to know exactly what was going on.[43]

Nevertheless, she causes a great deal of harm within this comic framework. Once Schmidt and his daughter have seen through her, they are immune, but things are very different in Jenny's family. She forces her rather likable husband to stop his championing of the engagement. (Jenny is on very shaky ground here, for she herself has risen from a far lower station than Corinna's; but her husband is so much under her sway that, after winning one victory, he capitulates.) Leopold's case is much worse. Without wishing to overstress psychoanalytic insights, one cannot help seeing him as the victim of a castrating female, of Mom—*Die Frau Mama*—writ large.

But again, this is comedy. Not literally emasculated, Leopold will marry a rich little snip from Hamburg and no doubt lead a reasonably unhappy life; however, all that lies outside the book. It has been pointed out that Jenny Treibel does not dominate the novel, despite its title.[44] If she did, the book might have been a great satire on the bourgeois world of *Bildung und Besitz* (culture and material wealth), but its comic quality would have been vitiated. This quality derives largely from the characteristic abundance of conversations. Fontane has not only his usual dinner and *Landpartie* scenes, but a chapter devoted to a stag evening given by the professor for his colleagues; he presents a wide range of social types, including ladies of the nobility, the Schmidts' old servant, and a traveling Englishman. Almost all of them, even Jenny at times, are either amusing in themselves or a cause of amusement in others. Broadly speaking, *Frau Jenny Treibel* has not dated: it is relevant today to any prosperous class or group—not only in the more or less capitalistic countries—in which human values have been subordinated to material ones.

Effi Briest

Fontane's most renowned novel, *Effi Briest* (1895), is in many ways his finest. He was usually oppressed by the work of revision and complained that inspiration only "dribbled out," but he wrote that in this case everything went painlessly, as in a dream.[45] In structure *Effi Briest* is classical: there are no extraneous episodes or anecdotes; Effi is always at the center of interest, even when she is "off stage"; all the secondary figures are carefully subordinated to her.[46] Further, the novel's symbols unobtrusively reinforce its central meaning: they say what the plot says, in different terms. *Effi Briest* is concerned with a "classic" situation of the nineteenth-century novel: the woman between husband and lover. Hence, it has often been compared to *Madame Bovary*, *Anna Karenina*, and *The Elective Affinities*.[47] (This seems to me rather like comparing a very fine artist of not quite the first rank to a towering genius: Ibsen to Shakespeare, perhaps, or Schubert to Beethoven.) Another favorite topic of nineteenth-century literature—treatment of a woman as a child or a thing—is important but not central; Fontane's approach to feminism, and to "problems" as such, was very different from Ibsen's.

While *Effi Briest* is largely dramatic in its presentation, Fontane did not depend as heavily on conversation here as in *Frau Jenny Treibel* or in *Der Stechlin*. After all, Effi could not discuss her "fall" with anyone, and he thought it tasteless to record intimate scenes in fiction. Accordingly, he relied a good deal on monologue and *erlebte Rede*—the technique of rendering a character's thoughts in the third person, but not in conventional indirect discourse, as in the sentence "Tomorrow he would go to London." Thus Effi reflects:

> That Innstetten had a ghost handy in order to keep his house from being completely ordinary was forgivable; it went with his tendency to be different from the crowd; but the other point, that he was using this ghost as a way of training her, that was nasty, almost insulting.[48]

Near the end, the narrator's sympathy for the dying heroine is so great that he drops all attempts at objectivity and addresses her directly as "poor Effi" (p. 370). On the whole, however, the action could stand on its own;[49] explanations and comments may be helpful but are not really necessary.

In *Effi Briest*, Fontane's mastery of various stylistic devices is at its height. It has often been noted how the words "Effi, come!" frame the story; we hear it in the opening scene, and it is the text of the telegram her parents send her when they finally relent. Old Briest's much cited remark, "That is too broad a field," serves as a humorous leitmotif and also to suggest a typically Fontanean quality: the awareness that many matters are too complicated or enigmatic to be profitably discussed. Less obvious is Fontane's use of anticipation. Effi tells her mother, before her marriage, that the one thing she cannot stand is boredom. On a much later occasion, when Innstetten has jokingly referred to Don Juan, Crampas suddenly appears. There are various other instances. (Thomas Mann seems to have learned a great deal of his anticipatory technique from Fontane. In

Buddenbrooks, chapters tend to end with pregnant remarks; after describing, for example, the weary manner and "decadent" beauty of Thomas Buddenbrook's fiancée, he closes with the sentence: "It was Gerda, the mother of future Buddenbrooks.") Fontane also makes use of parallelism: Effi's devoted servant, Roswitha, has a "past" herself; when a group in Kessin plans to put on an amateur performance, the play selected (by Crampas) is *Ein Schritt vom Wege* ("The Misstep").

Effi is introduced in a scene of great charm, probably Fontane's finest exposition, as a girl of seventeen, still almost a child, playing with three girls of about her own age. A bit of a tomboy, she likes swings, climbing, skating—any sport which gives the sense of soaring or flying. This trait is so persuasively shown that we do not at once recognize its symbolic overtones: a love of danger[50] and a certain flightiness in her. Her boldness appears in her "unladylike," at times mildly suggestive remarks, which her friends find shocking (or affect to); but she is actually very feminine, very attractive—and remarkably immature.

Thus it comes as a considerable shock when one reads, after a very few pages, that Baron von Innstetten, who at thirty-eight is over twice her age, has proposed marriage; that Effi's mother has strongly urged her to accept; and that she has done so almost at once. (We have already learned that Innstetten was once in love with Frau von Briest, and this casually imparted bit of information adds to our uneasiness.) Clearly this is a risky sort of match; but it is excessive, I think, to consider Effi's consent to the marriage a betrayal of her innermost nature.[51] While her mind is anything but complex, her nature is; and one of its components is a frankly admitted desire for success and prestige, which Innstetten seems—and is—destined to achieve.

On the other hand, as Fontane has already shown us, she loves adventure and "romances" and fears boredom; this side of her character she does indeed betray.

Apparently Effi's mother is in part to blame for the girl's excessive devotion to rank and wealth. Frau von Briest's values are as external as Jenny Treibel's, but they are not hypocritically concealed. In any case Effi, young and excited by the prospect before her though she is, has forebodings: she feels that Innstetten is a "man of principle," as indeed he is, for better and especially for worse. Effi's father has also sensed that there is something very dubious about the engagement; and her mother, whose common sense helps to offset her less attractive qualities, is worried, foreseeing that Effi will be bored.

So much for the exposition; Fontane establishes the situation in a very few pages, less than fifty in the standard edition. Slightly more than half of the book deals with Effi's life with Innstetten in the Baltic seaport town of Kessin. Over six years of their ensuing married life in Berlin are sketched in very rapidly; then Innstetten's discovery of the letters sent Effi by her lover years before destroys the marriage; the fatal duel and the divorce are briefly noted. The last two sections, both brief, are devoted to Effi's "exile" as a divorcée and her last days at her family's estate, after they have "forgiven" her. The first clear indication of her adultery comes about halfway through the book.

To return to Effi's married life: she is welcomed pleasantly enough to Kessin, but during her first night there she is disturbed by mysterious noises; people believe the house is haunted, and Innstetten is evasive when she tries to have the matter cleared up. It is most improbable that Fontane believed in ghosts, but the incident tells us a great deal about husband and wife, and indirectly, as we shall see, it helps to make plausible Effi's affair with Major Crampas. Further, the suggestion of the uncanny serves to increase one's sense of apprehension about Effi's marriage.

The reactions of the people she meets in and around Kessin illuminate other sides of her personality; we see her mirrored in their eyes.[52] If she often appears a good deal more childish than Ibsen's Nora, so that Innstetten's treatment of her is understandable, her actions in society reveal her attractive side. "Contacts" are pitifully few: there are a group of cultivated burghers in the town, centered on the eccentric apothecary Alonso Gieshübler, and a few noble families in the surrounding country. That Gieshübler, the most amusing figure in the book, is devoted to Effi, adds to her charm in our eyes; that the incredibly bigoted old maid, Sidonie von Grasenabb, detests her, is an equally good sign. Similarly, the reactions of servants, casual acquaintances, and even of Innstetten's dog brighten her "image."

Why, we ask, does Effi "fall"? Not from love, like Anna Karenina, nor from Emma Bovary's sensuality. Major Crampas is handsome and agreeable but not overwhelmingly so; he does not sweep Effi away but gradually wears down her resistance.[53] He is amoral, rather a playboy, but, at least in contrast to Innstetten, unconventional and amusing. Like Effi, he likes to take chances, and his reputation as a dangerous man where women are involved seems to add to his attractiveness. More important, Effi is hurt that Innstetten, even after the birth of their daughter, treats her like a child, that he often neglects her for the sake of his career, and above all, that he has not behaved more kindly in the matter of the ghost. Crampas very shrewdly points out that Innstetten is using the story of the ghost to keep her in a state of anxiety, in effect to isolate her from potential lovers. Although she tries not to accept this analysis, which of course is a flagrant betrayal of Innstetten, Crampas' old friend, Effi feels that there is truth in it and is spirited enough to resent it fiercely. Boredom and resentment are plausible rather than creditable motives, but the reason for her anger is not ignoble.

It has been shown that there are all sorts of parallels and similarities, great and small, between *Effi Briest* and *Madame Bovary*, extending even to the fact that both heroines in their loneliness turn to their dogs for comfort. Very probably Fontane knew *Madame Bovary*, though apparently he does not mention it.[54] In crucial matters, however, the differences are far more important than the similarities. Whatever Effi says or does, however silly, has *style*. She is immature but basically attractive, *sympathique;* Emma Bovary is the reverse. If Effi is like a Persian kitten which strays into serious mischief, Emma is a formidable alley cat. The tone of the author, in both cases, is appropriate to the character of his protagonist.

Friedrich Spielhagen and others have argued that Effi would not have kept the incriminating letters for so long a time: however naïve she may have remained, she wants desperately to forget the affair and is still afraid that it will come to light.[55] There are two possible answers to this criticism. First, Fontane believed that there is a mysterious connection between guilt and the "unfortunate coincidences" which—"not always, but often"—later befall the guilty person.[56] Second, I suggest that Effi unconsciously wants the truth to come out. Normally frank, she almost gives herself away to Innstetten, and she speaks to her servant Roswitha about the happiness of making a confession (pp. 224, 229); but knowing that her husband is a "man of principle," she does not dare to confide in him. To the objection that this explanation smacks of twentieth-century psychology, I would reply that Freudian slips have been recorded since the days of the Greeks.

Although Effi feels at times a strong sense of guilt, she admits in an important monologue that actually it is anxiety and fear, not awareness of sin, which oppress her. She is less ashamed of her adultery than of the lying involved: "I was always proud that I couldn't lie and did not need to; lying is so vulgar" (p. 272). Accordingly, she realizes that from a conventionally moral point of view she does not feel "real" remorse or shame.

Some years after the divorce, Effi obtains Innstetten's reluctant permission to see their daughter again. The child visits her mother, but the reunion is a dreadful fiasco; she has been so much influenced by her father that she is totally estranged. She replies only with a repeated "O certainly, if I may," to all of Effi's suggestions for further meetings. After the child has left, Effi breaks into a rage, her only real outburst. Innstetten's rigid pharisaism is far worse, she feels, than her own offense: "What I did, sickens me, but what sickens me more, is your virtue" (pp. 347–348). Here Effi assumes the defiant tone of an Ibsenian heroine, a note which neither she nor the narrator strikes elsewhere; but under the circumstances it is quite in character. On the whole, while Effi gains new insights, she does not really change a great deal. Shortly before her death, she states her final opinion of Innstetten in words which typically combine generosity and frankness: "There was a great deal of good in him, and he was as noble as anyone can be who is without genuine love" (p. 372). At her request, only her maiden name is inscribed on her gravestone.

Since we are led to identify ourselves with Effi's point of view, Innstetten appears as a basically unpleasant person.

This he may be—"a tinkling brass and a clanging cymbal" —but his Prussian rigidity is as much the product of his milieu and education as Effi's faults are the result of hers. Not that Fontane was a determinist; but his books show the importance of environment: it does not account for everything, but for a great deal. In a letter written not long after the publication of *Effi Briest*, he noted his wry amusement that some readers condemned Innstetten because of his correctness; actually he was a fine fellow with many lovable qualities.[57] It is hard to take this literally, for the book itself leads us to judge Innstetten severely: we feel that a man of his intelligence and experience should behave differently. Fontane emphasized his stature by making him a trusted adviser and protégé of Bismarck himself; Innstetten should then be self-confident enough not to base his behavior on "what other people might think." When he realizes this, it is far too late. Just as his guilt is greater than Effi's, his punishment is harsher—I am not imputing "poetic justice" to Fontane—and the dreariness of his life makes his professional success a mockery in his own eyes.

Aside from the strange matter of the ghost, Innstetten does not appear as actually a bad or neglectful husband. In that instance he treats Effi quite cruelly, perhaps because he is unsure of his own position vis-à-vis his young and beautiful wife. (The book is rather unclear as to whether or not Innstetten believes in "spooks"; but when he tells Effi, after they have left Kessin, that although such things exist, he does not believe in "their" ghost, there seems no reason to doubt him.) In fact, he is not as strong or self-confident as he appears. In connection with Innstetten's enthusiasm for Wagner, Fontane notes that some observers attributed it to his bad nerves, others to the composer's anti-Semitism. "Probably both parties were right" (p. 125)—an apparently trivial touch which makes us see that this highly promising civil servant is actually rather neurotic. Yet there is no doubt that he loves Effi "in his own fashion." If sometimes he puts his career before his wife, that is part of the implied bargain between the two: Effi is as eager for his success as he is.

When, however, Innstetten decides that he must fight a duel with Crampas, even though the affair lies so far in the past that he feels neither angry nor revengeful, he runs the risk of losing our sympathy completely. The dialogue in which he discusses the matter with his confidant Wüllersdorf is the moral center of the novel. Wüllersdorf makes the sensible point that if Innstetten kills Crampas, his unhappiness will be even greater; a duel would be justified only as the inevitable expression of wounded emotion. Then Innstetten counters by citing the moral code of his class, even claiming that the mere act of confiding in his friend has compromised his honor. The latter capitulates so easily that one feels Fontane has loaded the dice: "I find it dreadful that you're right, but you *are*. . . . Our cult of honor is idolatry, but we must submit to it as long as the idol is worshipped" (p. 297). We "must submit" to what we know to be untrue. Innstetten's offense does not consist of the duel as such but of obedience to a code in which he did not believe.[58] One is reminded of later German officers, otherwise decent, led by their purely formal concept of honor to play the part of the Devil's general.

After he has killed Crampas, Innstetten, as well he might, feels like a murderer: he cannot forget the look in the eyes of the dying man. At least he admits to himself, and later to Wüllersdorf, that his action was neither noble nor necessary. The rest of his life is dust and ashes, and his confidant can only recommend stoic endurance complemented by small epicurean pleasures—"auxiliary constructions," as he calls them. Presumably Innstetten will behave more humanely because of his bitter lesson, but that is very cold comfort.

In his portrayal of Innstetten, Fontane seems to have sensed the threat of decay in the new empire, despite all its military glory and strength. (Thomas Mann's *Death in Venice* conveys the same sense, but Mann had the perspective gained by writing almost twenty years later.) Innstetten, like Gustav von Aschenbach, is superficially a resolute, admirable figure; actuality is different. His concept of duty has little if any relation to Kant's—the categorical imperative is not based on "what other people may think." The old Prussian traditions are decaying; no viable new ethic has been found to replace them. None of this is stated; it is implied, and Fontane does not claim to be a philosopher of history or a moralist; when he is one, it is *malgré lui*. While his predeliction for smart officers and the military in general can be irritating, it is not sinister. Underneath he knew better.

In conclusion, a question concerning the title of the novel may give an inkling of its general intention. Why is it not "Effi *von* Briest"? Effi had a great deal of family pride, and Fontane was partial to the nobility, at least for literary purposes. Further, Effi does possess certain genuinely aristocratic virtues—courage, honesty, style—along with some of the shortcomings associated with her class. One reason, perhaps, is that Effi is, or has become, unpretentious like her father. The main point is that the book is not, for all its social detail, primarily about a woman of a certain class but about a human being.

Der Stechlin

Often referred to as his "novel of old age," *Der Stechlin* appeared in late 1898, a few months after Fontane's death.[59] Of course none of his narratives was written when he was young, but the tag is not useless. The book deals largely with the declining years and death of Dubslav von Stechlin, with whom Fontane often almost identifies himself; and it is less concerned with action and passion than with reflections on politics, religion, and life in general. Even more than *Die Poggenpuhls*, this is a work in which "how" has largely replaced "what." It is uncharacteristically long—over five hundred pages—and contains so many conversations that it could be called garrulous—although agreeably so. There is a tendency toward duplication: *two* visits to Stechlin's castle are presented at length, and there are *two* wise old men. (Herr von Barby, Stechlin's opposite number, shares many of his attitudes.) While there are many scenes of great verisimilitude, Fontane is less concerned than before with the conventions of realism. Thus Lake Stechlin, we are told, is mysteriously linked to volcanoes all over the world; when there is an eruption in Iceland or Java, a waterspout is formed on its surface. (As will appear, Fontane used this legend for symbolic purposes; such improbabilities no longer disturbed him.) Similarly, the young woman who grasps instinctively the symbolic importance of the lake is given the name of a water nymph—Melusine.

It is not the case that "nothing happens" in the novel. Thus Stechlin's son Woldemar chooses between two sisters, marries, and will carry the family tradition farther. There is no shortage of characters: the friends von Rex and von Czako, who are neatly contrasted, as are Melusine and her sister Armgard von Barby; the usual eccentrics, often with comic names; a *nouveau riche* couple; and many others. Fontane now appears to be less interested than before in preserving distance or neutrality: we are told bluntly that Stechlin's sister dislikes anything which suggests beauty or freedom to her mind. Basically this is a novel of ideas; action as such is subordinated to the themes discussed. Woldemar von Stechlin is a rather dim figure; it is the thinkers and conversationalists—especially Dubslav, the liberal Pastor Lorenzen, and Melusine—whom we remember. The topics of conversation are important in themselves; discourse here is more than a social pastime. Conversely, the manner of talking is rooted in character; we do not have imaginary dialogues carried on by faceless persons.

Before turning to the themes of *Der Stechlin*, we should consider the book's protagonist. Dubslav's views are a mixture of the extremely conservative—he is a Junker after all—with the liberal; the latter prevails. There is something of the eighteenth century about him. Like Fontane, he is basically a skeptic, of the tolerant, not the bitter, sort. If he believes that there are "no indisputable truths," he upholds certain attitudes unswervingly: "Conceit and arrogance . . . were about the only things which infuriated him" (p. 6). His skepticism is very far from nihilism.[60] It is typical that he gives as his reason for not remarrying—he was widowed young—his fear of cutting a ridiculous figure in heaven with two wives. (Actually, he does not believe in the resurrection of the body.) Characteristically, he can admire both Russian czars and the Social Democratic party. If his views are unduly eclectic, his character is winning; although anything but stuffy, he is proud of belonging to an old if somewhat impoverished family, which he considers quite as good as the Bismarcks or the Hohenzollerns. He seems to be that sort of nobleman who can accept new ideas and social forces gracefully. (His sister incarnates the "know-nothing" type of Junker; Fontane's attitude toward her is made clear early in the story.) Dubslav is a partisan neither of the old nor of the new; the type of aristocracy he represents, Fontane indicates, can form a valuable part of the era which is coming.

When Fontane called *Der Stechlin* political, he was using the term very broadly, to include social behavior and ethics.[61] Thus there is an indissoluble link between politics and religion: Pastor Lorenzen—an old friend of Stechlin and the mentor of his son Woldemar—is deeply concerned with political and especially social matters; his ideas are closer to the intention of the book than are the protagonist's. Just as Fontane can express admiration of Frederick the Great without championing the "good old days," he (and the book) distinguish between healthy forces in the present and those which are sinister or comic. Again, the theme of the new versus the old is central.

When young Woldemar champions the new spirit, Lorenzen replies that men should uphold "the old as long as it functions decently, and the new only as far as necessary" (p. 35). Perhaps he is leaning over backward to avoid offending the others present. Melusine later formulates the matter differently: "We should love everything old insofar as it deserves it, but it is for the new that we should really live" (pp. 361–362). As one would expect, neither liberals nor conservatives have a monopoly of virtue or of Fontane's sympathies. Thus the Social Democratic politician Torgelow is a charlatan, but the party itself is referred to with respect. While Stechlin is delightful, most of his fellow Junkers are rather unprepossessing, and his reactionary sister Adelheid is referred to as "petrified" and "prehistoric." Old Stechlin's philippic against modern tendencies, when he is near death, loses most of its sting because it is basically good-humored. Feeling that his son's generation is unduly catholic in its tastes, he lists its heroes:

> old Wilhelm and Kaiser Friedrich and Bismarck and Moltke, and Mazzini and Garibaldi in between them, very friendly-like, and Marx and Lassalle—at least they were dead—and Bebel and Liebknecht next to them. And then Woldemar says: "Look at Bebel. My political opponent, but a man of character" [p. 497].

Old Stechlin would himself admit that a political opponent could be decent; his point here is that the liberal pantheon is too inclusive, and he is not entirely wrong. To Pastor Lorenzen, the real heroes of the present are the inventors and explorers.

The relations among the various social classes and the tensions within them also appear as elements of the general dialectics of present versus past. Three years before *Der Stechlin* was finished, Fontane wrote to a friend that the book would be concerned with "the contrast between the nobility as it ought to be and as it is." [62] As has been noted,[63] this is not a major theme of the finished novel, but the opposition between the enlightened nobles Stechlin and Barby (and their children) on the one hand and Adelheid's circles on the other is very clear. As usual, servants and other members of the "lower" classes appear in a very favorable light, but in this explicitly political novel, Fontane goes further and speaks of the fourth estate. In one of the book's numerous conversations, the intelligent Czech Dr. Wrschowitz describes the Berlin population in one lapidary sentence: "Upper class good, lower class very good; middle class not very good" (p. 310). Again, the bourgeoisie could hardly be worse, and the newly ennobled Herr von Gundermann, with his freshly acquired ultraconservative views, is equally unattractive. Unlike the Junker families, the rich burghers show no sense of *noblesse oblige* in dealing with their servants.

A similar dichotomy between old and new appears in religious matters. The likable characters, especially Stechlin, Lorenzen, and Armgard von Barby, are decidedly Christian in their ethics and basic attitudes, though Stechlin is anything but orthodox, and Lorenzen, despite his calling, seems to be even less so. The "party-line" Christians like Adelheid von Stechlin are intolerably intolerant, whereas Armgard, who is not particularly pious, instinctively prefers St. Elizabeth to Queen Elizabeth: helping the poor is the highest ideal, she feels. It is as if socialism were invoked to take the curse off dogmatic Christianity, and Christianity were to perform the same function for doctrinaire socialism. Some sort of Christian socialism, then, would seem to be an integral part of the synthesis to which the book points. When Lorenzen reassures Stechlin that the new Christianity is identical with the old, he recalls the early Christians who "had all things in common" and preserves the novel's Fontanean balance between past and present.

If the term "Christian Socialism" has a somewhat ambiguous ring today, that is largely the fault of Adolf Stoecker, court preacher at Berlin from 1874 to 1889. However sincere Stoecker may have been in his efforts to win back the working classes to Christianity by preaching a highly conservative sort of "social gospel," he is now mainly remembered for his propagation of anti-Semitism. Fontane realized that Lorenzen's social aims would remind his readers of Stoecker's, and he mentions the actual pastor in the novel in order to differentiate between the two types. It is characteristic of Fontane's realism that he brings in a number of contemporary figures from Bismarck down, while he is very careful to preserve the privacy of ordinary citizens.[64] It is also typical that he does not mention Stoecker's anti-Semitism, not (I believe) because the theme was taboo but because it was beneath contempt. He wrote to Friedrich Paulsen that the novel tended to uphold the ideas of Stoecker and the Social-Democratic leader August Bebel in ennobled form, rather than the Prussian ideal.[65] Lorenzen and the other champions of "the new" are not expressly committed to any specific economic or social reforms; their socialism is based on the New Testament, not on the class struggle.[66]

Quite clearly, the symbol of Lake Stechlin is the key to understanding the book's political drift. As will be recalled, when a volcano erupts anywhere in the world, a waterspout is formed; during really great catastrophes, a red rooster also appears. Doubtless, the volcanoes and earthquakes, as in Goethe's *Faust*, symbolize revolutions; it has been plausibly suggested that the red rooster—the Gallic cock?—points to France.[67] In other words, even the most rural, remote parts of Prussia are inextricably linked, like Germany as a whole, to the rest of the world: Adelheid and the other reactionaries are wrong, for no country is immune to change. Although there is something frightening about the lake,[68] what it symbolizes is basically beneficent. Further, the lake preserves its character throughout the centuries—not despite these occasional "revolutions" but because of them.[69]

If this interpretation is correct, the novel must be largely acquitted of any charge of ambivalence. Much of Stechlin's charm derives from the fact that he usually transcends the prejudices of his class. Not that Fontane was or claimed to be an activist. His own attitude recalls that of Professor Schmidt, in *Frau Jenny Treibel*, who tells his daughter that he would join the Social Democrats—if he were not a professor. Yet *Der Stechlin* remains rewarding for its theme as well as its style, for "what" as well as "how." Whether or not one attaches the label "late" to the novel, it has a special character, an appeal of its own.

2/ An Unsentimental Education: Robert Musil's *Young Törless*

"Where Id was, shall Ego be."
—Sigmund Freud

To encounter Robert Musil among the Central European writers of the earlier twentieth century is a refreshing surprise: none of the clichés applies to him. He is not romantic, not sentimental; he does not make a cult of youth, music, the soul, or nature. No "mere rationalist," he was keenly aware of the depths of the unconscious; this very awareness made him all the more convinced of the value and necessity of logic and clarity. One might call him the anti–Hermann Hesse. Differently put: coming across one of his books after reading, say, the early stories of Hesse or Werfel is almost like meeting Voltaire at a conference of anthroposophists.

To be sure, Musil was no isolated phenomenon. Although Vienna was a center of neoromanticism in literature, music, and painting around the turn of the century, there were countervailing tendencies: the names of Freud, Schnitzler, Mach, and Wittgenstein spring to mind. Musil was trained as an engineer and a mathematician and wrote a dissertation on Mach. Precision and detachment characterize all his work. Yet he was well aware that only one hemisphere of life had proved accessible to scientific methods. He was obsessed by the hope, Utopian as he called it, of achieving a combination and interpenetration of rational and nonrational elements—not a "synthesis" in the bombastic Hegelian sense. A "secretariat of precision and soul" was one of his formulas for this quest. In other words, the "night side" of life, the irrational elements, the emotions and intuitions, are not to be underrated—Musil was as convinced of their importance as were Rilke and Hofmannsthal—but to be explored, accurately and coolly. Sober observation, not "dialectics," and mathematics, not *Geistesgeschichte*, are needed. Of the twentieth-century German writers known to me, Musil is the closest to Freud in lucidity of thought and intellectual courage.

Of course this great combination is the major theme of Musil's enormous but never finished *The Man without Qualities* (1930–1942). It also figures importantly in his other novel, *Young Törless* (1906). Since the latter book, somewhat overshadowed by its giant successor, is fascinating both in itself and as a pioneering work of fiction, it is worth discussing in its own right. *Törless* is amazingly ahead of its time in its subtlety of psychological analysis, its freedom from both sentimentality and sensationalism, and its frank treatment of sexual matters, including in this case homosexuality and sadism. Although less brilliant than *The Man without Qualities*, it is formally far more successful: in Musil's magnum opus the essayistic sections tend to overwhelm the book as well as the reader.

Young Törless is essentially the analysis of a critical period in the life of an adolescent. Törless, sixteen years old, is a student at an aristocratic military academy, located in the eastern flatlands of the Austro-Hungarian Empire, not far from the Russian border. His experiences are extremely unpleasant, in fact potentially ruinous, but he survives: he is a brilliant, sensitive but not a weak youth. (Presumably there is some autobiographical substructure.) *Törless* has something in common with the traditional *Bildungsroman*, but its protagonist, basically a realist, is no Wilhelm Meister or Parzival. Similarly, while the theme of *Törless* links it to the "school novel" of the period, which depicted the sufferings inflicted on defenseless boys by unfeeling schoolmasters, its tone is radically different. Musil has not written an emotional protest against the educational establishment, as Hesse did in *Unterm Rad* (*The Prodigy*) and Emil Strauss in *Freund Hein*, nor a satire like Heinrich Mann's *Professor Unrat* (*Small Town Tyrant*). Musil's aim was rather to describe, *sine ira et studio*, the ordeal of Törless. Clearly, the narrator's sympathies are with his hero, but he does not load the dice. The threat to Törless does not come from the school as such, but partly from contemporary society as reflected in his companions, still more from forces within himself. He is changed; to some extent he "grows up"; but this is an educational novel with a difference. Possibly the protagonist's name is symbolic: he becomes less of a fool, is partially rid of folly—*der Torheit los*. Perhaps the closest analogy—though not a very close one—is Joyce's *Portrait of the Artist as a Young Man*.

There are two levels of action: the external, dealing with Törless' psychological "confusions," and the internal, concerned with his intellectual adventures. Actually the two planes merge into one. Whenever Törless is really stirred, whether by an attractive body or such an enigmatic concept as the square root of minus one, he feels a thrill which Musil clearly links to sexual excitement.[1] To Törless a challenging mathematical concept is as stirring as an erotic adventure. Not more so: he is not unduly bookish and regards his teachers (who are his social and intellectual inferiors) with a mixture of contempt, pity, and curiosity.

On the literal level, the action centers on Törless' relations with three of his schoolmates: Beineberg, Reiting, and Basini. The first two, larger and somewhat older than the protagonist, attract him partly because of their bad reputations: he is bored and has yet to develop any real independence of character (p. 21). Basini, a miserable youth, is completely in the power of Reiting and Beineberg, who have found out about a theft he committed and blackmail him ruthlessly. He is their slave, the object of their sadistic and homosexual aggressions. Reluctantly fascinated, Törless observes their "experiments" and for a while takes some part in them.

Musil's characterization contrasts the two bullies very strikingly. Beineberg is a pretentious pseudo intellectual, sincere but hopelessly unbalanced, in a sense even stupid. Unfortunately, this type occurred all too often in what one might call the Wagner-through-Hitler period of German culture, as the criticisms raised by Heinrich and Thomas Mann, Karl Kraus, Broch, and Musil himself attest. Musil preserved several further examples in *The Man without Qualities*, "like flies in amber." Beineberg's father, who had spent some time in India, returned filled with an unrequited passion for the wisdom of the East. In his turn, the youth has picked up and exaggerated his father's obsession. Convinced that fakirs can suspend the laws of nature, he tries to induce "mystical" states of mind in poor Basini, by torture as well as hypnotism.

Reiting, for his part, is devoted to power for its own sake: he is a completely unscrupulous "operator," whose greatest pleasure lies in intrigue. When the mood takes him, he stirs up trouble quite gratuitously. As clever (in his way) as he is cruel, he deduces Basini's theft from circumstantial evidence and browbeats him into confession. His comment is typical: "There is nothing finer than when a man suddenly reveals himself like this, and his whole way of life, unnoticed before, is suddenly exposed like the tunnelings of a worm when a piece of wood breaks in two" (pp. 50–51). Reiting believes that he is mysteriously related to a "very lofty family" and dreams of *coups d'état.* As one would expect, he makes a great cult of Napoleon. Like Beineberg, he enjoys torturing Basini mentally and physically and abusing him sexually. The unpleasant pair is especially dangerous to Törless, in that each possesses, in a distorted form, characteristics of the protagonist: Beineberg has Törless' intellectual speculations, Reiting his ambition.

If Beineberg with his "philosophizing" seems to anticipate figures like Alfred Rosenberg and Hitler himself, Reiting suggests the opportunistic, activistic type of Nazi—men like Goering or Ernst Röhm. (Probably the latter sort is a bit less despicable.) Basini completes the vicious circle: the predestined victim, soft, masochistic, weak rather than evil. Although Musil himself wrote that *Törless* foreshadowed National Socialism,[2] I do not believe that he specifically foresaw, in the first years of the twentieth century, the rise of German Fascism. Rather, he was aware, as few if any others were at the time, that there were forces in contemporary Austria which pointed toward sadistic tyranny. The secret room where Beineberg's and Reiting's activities are focused is located "like a forgotten relic of the Middle Ages, away from the warm, clear life of the classrooms" (p. 112). In its threatening archaism it suggests the unconscious mind but has political overtones as well.[3] Reiting likes "mass movements" (p. 121), because each member of a mob eggs the others on to violence; and this is exactly what transpires when the cadets, inflamed by the two sadists, join in the attack on Basini. After an earlier beating, the poor wretch howls like a dog. Besides the other services he performs, he has to read aloud to Reiting—bloodthirsty episodes about the Borgias, the later Roman emperors, and so on. Even when the whole disgrace has come to light, the students unite to put all the blame on Basini, who is expelled. As Robert Minder remarks, this final turn of the screw anticipates the attitude of many Nazis in 1945: the guilty testify to each other's innocence.[4]

In this sense, many details in *Törless* do indeed have a prophetic ring today. Of course it could plausibly be objected that German boarding schools are no more notorious for sadism and homosexuality than non-Teutonic ones. The secret room with its red walls, however, is another matter: it seems *echt deutsch*. Musil's account is by no means implausible: it is representative of many German schools and academies, though of course not of all.[5]

Törless is narrated almost entirely in the third person.[6] Although we often perceive the cadets and their doings through the eyes of the hero, a highly intelligent adolescent, the narrator sometimes steps away from the story, as it were, to comment on it. At one point we are told of a development which took place years after Törless' "confusions" were things of the past: "Later, after Törless had surmounted (*überwunden*) the events of his youth, he became a young man of very subtle and sensitive intellect" (p. 118). At a few points the narrator ventures a generalization. When Törless, hearing of the plan to "punish" Basini, feels a shiver of cold, we read, "People say that a man has this sensation when he first sees the woman destined to involve him in a ruinous passion" (p. 53). Later, Basini's presence has a physical impact on Törless "like sleeping beside a woman whom one can uncover at any time" (p. 100).

Musil's opening words suggest the mood and the milieu: "A little station on the line that leads to Russia." The four parallel rails seem to extend endlessly; the scorched earth around them is "like a dirty shadow"; the trees are dismal, parched, their leaves "throttled by dust and soot"; the colors of the landscape are drab; the light of the afternoon sun is "pale" (p. 15). The school seems to be located at the rim of civilization, in the "middle of nowhere." In some ways, *Törless* is, as Frank Kermode put it, a "gloomy" novel,[7] but its total impact is not depressing. To be sure, Musil's famous wit plays only a small part in the book, though there are a few epigrammatic flashes. Rather, Törless survives his sordid entanglements relatively unscathed and is in fact strengthened by his brush with evil. When Törless, years later, tells a friend about his "confusions," he admits that the episode was degrading but does not feel ashamed. Instead, he values it for having preserved him from the illusion of an "all too secure and tranquil healthiness" (p. 119), from naïve smugness. Musil does not draw any specific moral conclusions; he seems to treat Törless' experiences as one might regard an unpleasant but not too serious illness. One is reminded of Menninger's remark that a patient who has emerged from a mental illness is stronger than he was before its onset. Although *Törless* is in a sense a *Bildungsroman*, its cool tone and relatively neutral point of view set it off from most educational novels.

Törless is realistic in the best sense, but it is far from naturalistic. Musil's "characteristic unity of intellectual exactness and metaphoric imagery" [8] largely realizes his hope of combining "precision and soul"—to cite Musil's own formulation. While he presents physical and psychological ugliness unflinchingly, his tone is not clinical. In a moment of unrest, Törless feels as if "opalescent lizards" were darting over the surface of his soul (p. 71). He characteristically compares the mathematician's use of unreal concepts to obtain valid results to "a bridge with only the two end piers, which one nevertheless crosses as safely as if it were complete" (p. 81). (The reader soon realizes that Törless is no average boy; he is in fact potentially a genius.) During a sleepless night, the quarter-hours slip by Törless' bed "like nurses in a hospital" (p. 90). Like Mann's Hans Castorp, he often takes stock of his ideas and experiences; he is compared to a fisherman who "senses . . . that he has caught rich prey in his net" but cannot lift it from the water (p. 45). Images of snakes and traps are appropriately important; their gloom is partially offset by lighter metaphors, like the reference to the mathematics teacher who lived in "daily concubinage" with his subject (p. 82). Burton Pike well writes of "tensed images" in *Törless:* the images are strained "to convey to the reader's intellect an impression of Törless' *feelings*, and the language itself is stretched almost to the limits of what language can do." [9]

Without the lucidity of its style and the translucence of its images, *Törless* would be far less impressive. Basically, though, it is a character study, done with great care but with equal economy of means. (The novel takes up only about 130 pages in Adolf Frisé's edition.) As Jean Duvignaud puts it, Musil's aim, apparently, was "to strip a consciousness of its veils without reducing it to the status of a thing, without replacing it by the intelligence of the commentator." [10] Obviously, it is easier to do this successfully if the consciousness in question is similar to the author's own. Musil is both close to his protagonist, in this sense, and at the same time emotionally detached. Again one is reminded of Joyce's *Portrait of the Artist as a Young Man.*

Three basic factors seem to dominate Törless' personality: his intellectual brilliance, his precarious situation as an adolescent, and his sense of the duality of life. As to the first: although he is badly handicapped by the lack of a humanistic education, he is keenly interested in putting down his experiences on paper. In line with Remy de Gourmont's aphorism, he tries to arrange his impressions in a system. At one point he starts a manuscript with the naïvely ambitious title "De natura hominum." His interest in behavior is very real and explains in large part the pull he feels, against strong inner resistance, to be present during the interrogations of Basini. It is mathematics which interests him most. When he tells Beineberg that a fresh thought causes "a start . . . , dizziness, a shock" (pp. 30–31), the latter dismisses the experience as intellectual gymnastics.[11] We are reminded of Tonio Kröger's attempt to interest his Philistine friend in Schiller. Later, after the mathematics teacher has cited Kant as an example of a thinker so difficult that beginners like Törless must accept his findings on faith, the boy goes out and buys the book in question. He even dreams of Kant. Although he can make little if anything of the philosopher, Kant is symbolically very relevant to Törless' (and Musil's) central questions: What is the relation between "precision" and "soul"? How does one get from one realm to the other, from phenomena to noumena?

Both his intellectual alertness and his sensitivity make him all the more vulnerable as an adolescent. Naturally, his trials are mainly concerned with sex, but they go beyond it. An only child, doted on by his parents, he is so impressionable that he "appear[s] to have no character at all" (p. 21). Musil well notes that unusual gifts tend to weaken, at a certain early stage, the self-confidence of their possessors—"for which reason youths with a great future usually have a past rich in humiliations" (p. 33). Törless was once terrified when a careless servant left him alone in the woods;

the trauma remains. Fastidious and extremely shy, he is actually more sensual than the average person. Although he believes consciously that his mother is the acme of sexless purity, he keeps thinking of her while he is in the room with the prostitute Bozena and is led to remember his mother's enigmatic laugh on evenings when his parents became unusually affectionate. It seemed "as if she were going, calmly, to close all the doors" (p. 43). A further cause of confusion is that the peasant girls and women with whom the older cadets flirt strike him as dirty, even bestial. (Up to this point he has fallen in love only once—with the voice of an unseen singer in a small Italian town.) Thus Törless is almost compelled to repress his normal sexual drive—and is made the more exposed to homoerotic attractions.

Yet this account, which may read almost like a clinical analysis so far, needs to be corrected. Törless is labile up to a point but has the faculty of regaining balance before his fall is complete. Thus while he is naturally afraid of Beineberg and Reiting, he fears them "only as one fears a giant who, one knows, is blind and stupid" (p. 57). When they threaten to reveal his part in the Basini affair, he is frightened, but not to the point of panic. (When he runs away, the threat of blackmail has already passed.) Earlier, at the moment of his extreme degradation, he felt: "This isn't me! . . . not really! . . . From tomorrow on I'll be myself again!" (p. 114). This may sound like a desperate rationalization, but subsequent events show that it is basically true. Toward the end of the story, he turns away from Basini with the—often necessary—cruelty of adolescence; but though he feels only hostility for the pathetic wretch, he does what he can to save him.

Törless' awareness of the antithetical nature of life is the main cause of his bewilderment: this duality includes the double aspect of sex—attraction and repulsion. Even as a child he felt that a "language of silence" existed. Although he was fascinated by words, he was aware of their inadequacy. "There is something dark in me, underneath all my thoughts," Törless tells the schoolmasters at the end, "something I can't measure with my thoughts, that can't be expressed in words and which is yet my life" (p. 143). (The book's motto, a quotation from Maeterlinck, makes the same point; it was a conviction shared by Hofmannsthal, Rilke, and many others.) Similarly, mathematical concepts are also inadequate, if in a different sense. Above all, the "other" world is linked to and affects the rational one: without imaginary numbers, mathematics would not function. Törless, like the protagonist of *The Man without Qualities* and like Musil himself, rejects all easy or superstitious explanations.

In large part, Törless becomes aware of the "split in the world"—as Kleist called it—through his confrontation with evil. If he could mingle thoughts of Bozena with memories of his mother, then anything was possible: Reiting, Beineberg, the secret room. Moreover, in society itself the boundary between "decent" people and the filthiest outcasts must be slight, a line one can cross at any moment. Hofmannsthal found a comparable if less drastic image for the bond between those who lie "with heavy limbs / By the roots of the confused life [*des verworrenen Lebens*]" and the others who live serenely, among the rulers:

> Doch ein Schatten fällt von jenen Leben
> In die anderen Leben hinüber,
> Und die leichten sind an die schweren
> Wie an Luft und Erde gebunden.[12]

Törless finally concludes that while "things" have two sides, one need not become confused by them. His final answer to the committee of teachers investigating the "Basini case" marks the end of his confusions: "I'm not afraid of anything any more. I know: things are things and will probably always be the way they are; and I'll probably always regard them now one way, now the other. Now with the eyes of the mind, now with the other ones" (pp. 143–144). Ironically, the director feels that Törless is so "overstimulated" that he should leave the school; he is given an honorable discharge, as it were. Now completely unconfused, the boy wishes to depart in any case. His mother, when she comes to take him home, is agreeably surprised by his calm self-possession. On the way to the station they pass the wood where Bozena's house stands. Now Törless, relatively adult, can think of his mother as another adult, not as a goddess of purity. He feels neither shame nor embarrassment.[13]

A final glance at the course of Törless' education may help to make clearer the reasons both for his entanglement and for his eventual self-extrication. He is not one of those of whom Thomas Mann wrote, "Some go astray because for them no right road exists." [14] Rather, he has intelligence and ambition, a favorable social position, and a relatively happy family background. If he is an "outsider," he is set apart only by his exceptional mind, which combines rational agility with sensitivity.

In Musil's eyes, the lack of a proper education was at least as serious a threat to Törless as was the atmosphere of the school. This opinion is based on very specific reasons of course; it is not the case that Musil had a stuffy or superstitious regard for "the great books" as a panacea. Deprived of the authors whom more fortunate Austrian boys read, willy-nilly, in school—Musil mentions Shakespeare, Goethe, Schiller, "and perhaps the moderns" (p. 20)—

Törless is alienated from a culture he is exceptionally qualified to understand. Therefore he accepts, at third hand, the belief of half-educated adults he has met:

> And Törless couldn't help thinking that the problems of philosophy had been finally solved by Kant and that it was senseless to concern oneself further with that subject; just as he believed that there was no point in writing poetry after Goethe and Schiller [p. 85].

(Spengler made the same specious point twelve years later in *The Decline of the West:* culture is no longer alive; all bright young men should take up technology.) So the "German classics" remain behind the glass doors of Father Törless' book cases, honored and unread in their "shrine," an "army of unalterable law"—to repeat Eliot's sarcastic quotation of a famous line. The boy's ambition is diverted from its proper aims, and he himself, frustrated and unsure of himself, is correspondingly more susceptible to the influence of others.

Under these circumstances, Törless' intellectual curiosity is a source of danger. Fortunately he is looking for "something natural" (p. 90) behind the paradoxes of mathematics; this search is an element of strength. He has no use for Beineberg's mystifications, noting that they would make no impression in broad daylight. Basini's ordeal fascinates him largely because of his disinterested—and very cold—inquisitiveness about human nature: What does extreme humiliation do to the personality? Before long he finds that his hope of making psychological discoveries has led him into a cramped, unhappy sensuality—"not from perversity but in consequence of a mental orientation which had no goal at the moment" (p. 120).

Once Törless has found the courage to break completely

with Beineberg and Reiting, he is able to put his perceptions about the duality of life into words, and thus to face it. Further, this intuition is now a "living" not a dead thought, as the narrator puts it; it has become existentially real.

> A great insight [*Erkenntnis*] takes place only half in the bright sphere of the brain, the other half in the dark ground of the innermost self; above all it is a state of the psyche in which the conscious thought appears only at the topmost point, like a blossom [pp. 142–143].

In this image Musil has attempted, to quote Pike again, "to convey through language mental processes which, partaking simultaneously of conscious and subconscious areas of mind, produce a blurred continuum of thought and nonverbal feeling." [15] Here Musil has certainly succeeded. By reproducing the "blurred continuum" he has achieved a paradoxically clear total effect.

Törless' final self-assertion is that of a young man who has emerged, not gloriously but decisively, from his first ordeal. There are hints that he may become a writer, a mathematician, perhaps a philosopher, but he is seen primarily as a gifted young man, not as "the artist." Doubtless there will be other confusions, but one senses that these will be more worthy of him. He has put the Beinebergs and Basinis behind him. By accepting and articulating his conviction that reality is Janus-faced, he has conquered his fear of it.

3/ Life as Nightmare: Franz Kafka's "A Country Doctor"

"This is too much for the human mind to grasp."
—Albert Einstein, on returning a volume
of Kafka to Thomas Mann

Anyone who tries to "explain" a story by Franz Kafka ought to make clear first on what guides and principles he relies in his quixotic, perhaps impossible quest. After all, Kafka himself stated, "All these metaphors (or symbols—*Gleichnisse*) aim only to convey that the incomprehensible is incomprehensible; and that we already knew."[1] The warning is salutary, but since Kafka was given to teasing the reader, and even more to making derogatory statements about his own work, one may, without disregarding the prohibition, refuse to bar all interpretation. When a sign says, "Road legally closed, proceed at your own risk," many of us do proceed—at our own risk.

To state then my presuppositions: Kafka's stories are fables[2] or parables of the human condition, not primarily of religion, the lot of the Jews, the Austro-Hungarian bureaucracy, or Freudian psychology—though any or all of these may be involved. There *is* no single, infallibly correct meaning to which we may reduce them. Rather, they are Aesopian[3] fables of an irrational, often tragic world, although they are sometimes wryly comic in tone. Like the fable of the fox and the grapes, they may be applied to a number of human situations. Normally, therefore, they suggest more than one valid application. At best, we can approximate, by repeated readings, the intention or intentions of one of Kafka's works. The stories which Kafka actually finished are marked by an extreme economy of means as well. Every word, every detail, even the change in the tense of a verb, may be highly important.

Very often Kafka's narratives follow a tripartite pattern: guilt, anxiety, punishment. Frequently, like "A Country Doctor," *The Trial*, and *The Metamorphosis*, they begin by plunging the hero into a crisis; reluctantly he becomes aware of the desperate seriousness of his predicament, of a guilt he cannot define yet struggles to deny. Generally this irruption of an inscrutable power crushes him, but until a man has confronted it, he does not truly exist. (One is reminded of Lichtenberg's "Non cogitant, ergo non sunt.") Thus, in the terms of "A Country Doctor," a wound is a dreadful fact, but not to be wounded is worse.

While Kafka's work bears the stamp of his unique style and *Weltanschauung*—he is one of the most individual of writers—his parables do share themes, traditions, and even characteristics of style with other writers. After all, they are part of literature, not monstrous sports; his style would have been different without the example of Heinrich von Kleist, his apposition of the panther to the "hunger artist" recalls Thomas Mann's antithesis of burghers and artists, and so on. Such studies as Erich Albert's,[4] which cites and compares country doctors in Turgenev, Flaubert, Balzac, and even Hans Carossa, are helpful if they are genuinely literary, not a mere recounting of sources and parallels.

A final "principle": Kafka's aphorisms may or may not cast light on a particular story of his. They belong to the philosophical rather than the aesthetic sphere, though often the two overlap. Such expressions of belief as the phrase "the indestructible in man" are of no help in reading the really black narratives, nor do the more characterstic aphorisms of despair, like "We are one of God's bad moods," illuminate "Josephine the Singer, or the Mouse People," a relatively lighthearted piece.

"A Country Doctor," Kafka wrote Max Brod, was a work he felt to be valid; [5] for him, this is exuberant self-praise. Written in the dark winter of 1916–1917, it became the title story of the collection he published in 1919 and dedicated to his father. If he really told a friend, as reported by Dora Gerritt, that this narrative consisted of variations on the terrors of the profession of medicine,[6] we may assume that he was deliberately (and typically) concealing a great deal.

Among the characteristics of "A Country Doctor," we first note that it is told in the first person. This is of course a clear reminder that we see events through the protagonist's eyes, not through those of a neutral narrator. (In the more typical stories told in the third person, the truth of what we learn is equally relative, although the reader is likely not to realize this.) [7] Yet paradoxically we do not identify ourselves more intimately with the doctor than with K. or Josef K., perhaps because so much of our sympathy is attracted first by Rose, later by the wounded boy.

Most striking of all is the effect of speed and breathlessness which the story conveys. Everything is told in one overlong paragraph, a device suggesting a sudden welling up of the subconscious. Although Kafka's precisely controlled style is normally far removed from that of his contemporaries the expressionists, he comes closer to them here than anywhere else. The reader seems to find himself in a dream or rather a nightmare, and is reminded of Charles

Neider's acute suggestion that "A Country Doctor" is possibly the rendering of a touched-up dream; "Kafka dreamed brilliantly," Neider points out.[8]

The story's logic is indeed that of a dream. Time expands and contracts; the action leaps wildly about; irrational, often impossible events take place: horses emerge from a pigsty; the physician is put to bed with his patient. Ambivalence prevails to a nightmarish extent: the boy at first has no wound, then a lethal one; although it is his wound, of course, it is insistently linked to Rose, largely through its color; the doctor at the end is ineffably alone, yet clearly aware of the doings of his patients and the machinations of his successor.

Perhaps because it so reminiscent of a dream, "A Country Doctor" is essentially symbolic. Night, snow, and cold determine the tone; the magic horses are significantly contrasted to the dead horse and later form a unit with the carriage, recalling the image of the charioteer in Goethe's *Egmont*. In this instance the allusion is literary rather than psychological. While the pigsty is an unambiguous symbol, the wound is far more complex. All the major characters are parabolic, standing for general types; Rose, with her significant name, is a key figure. That all the other persons are anonymous further emphasizes her importance.

Before turning to a close examination of the story, I would suggest a hypothetical reading, to be tested against the text: an interpretation of "A Country Doctor" as a surrealistic parable, using the pattern of a nightmare to represent man's fate in a wintry age. Like much of Kafka's other work, it shows the human condition as an enigmatically guilty one.

The story may be divided into four parts: the action up to the doctor's arrival at the cottage of his patients; his first encounter with the boy and his family; the discovery that the wound is real, with the consequences entailed; and the doctor's departure and fate. I shall attempt an explication of each part, and then a general conclusion.

Section 1. The doctor's account opens on a note of anxious urgency. A great deal is packed into the first, long, Kleistian sentence:

> I was in great embarrassment: I was confronted by an urgent journey; a seriously sick person was waiting for me in a village ten leagues away; heavy snowstorms filled the long stretch between me and him; I had a carriage, light, with big wheels, just the sort for our country roads; bundled in my fur coat, with my case of instruments in my hand, I was standing in the courtyard, ready to go; but the horse was lacking, the horse.[9]

So far, we have encountered nothing unreal; at most the repetition of "horse" at the end may seem hectic. The carriage horse has just died of overexertion; the servant girl has gone out into the cold to borrow a replacement. Although the physician knows that she will not succeed, he waits anyway—the first hint of the irrational. When the girl returns alone, she swings a lantern; this is in every sense a nocturnal tale. Nearby stands a decayed pigsty, unused for years; curiously, it is warm and smells of horses. A blue-eyed groom (villagers and servants are usually blond, Slavic types in Kafka) creeps out of it "on all fours." The girl remarks ambiguously, "People don't know what they have in their own houses." Perhaps the doctor has ignored her unduly. Two splendid horses, "Brother" and "Sister," crawl from the sty and stand upright. When the girl, obeying her employer, goes to help harness them, the groom makes a brutal attack on her. (With the words "embraces her" the tense suddenly shifts from the imperfect to the present;[10] the physician seems actually to be reliving the past.) The physician rebukes the groom fiercely—"You beast, do you want the whip?"—but does nothing. Ambivalent—we shall find that he is characteristically so—he fails the girl in this crisis and even gets "cheerfully" into the carriage. Rosa flees, but he is convinced that she is doomed. Our disgust at his betrayal is modified by the knowledge that the groom has more power than he: when the groom gives the horses the command "Lively!" and claps his hands, the carriage is "carried away like a piece of wood by the current." And the groom's desire to break open the door of the house seems equally irresistible. The speed and noise of the doctor's journey almost overwhelm him. In a moment he is at his patient's house, apparently a very modest one.

Interpretation. At first the physician seems more admirable than the traveling salesmen, bank officials, animals, and bugs who usually figure as Kafka's heroes; and to the extent that he actually does wish to help,[11] he indeed is. Presumably, mortally overstraining the horse was a concomitant of his own overwork. (Later on, he collapses completely.) What he was like before we shall never know; now, at any rate, he lacks authority and is plagued by anxiety. As a bachelor, he is per se guilty, in Kafka's terms. In overstressing his career, he has neglected the human element: he doesn't know what he has in his own house, to paraphrase Rosa. Even to save her from rape, he dare not risk living without a groom. Clearly he has repressed the emotional side of life; he is the type Schiller called a barbarian, not a real *Mensch*. Yet he seems to have treated Rose decently: she is clearly devoted to him. Apparently it is the aggressiveness of the groom that makes his latent weakness, his neurosis, evident.

The magic horses are not evil, but they are extremely

dangerous to a weakling. One thinks of the myth of Phaethon, and of the horses of the sun in *Egmont:*

As if whipped on by invisible spirits, the sun-horses of time run away with our fate's light chariot; and we have no choice, save to grasp the reins courageously and hold them firm, guiding the wheels now to the right, now to the left—from the rock here, the precipice there. Where we are going—who knows? He barely knows from where he came.[12]

In Plato's *Phaedrus,* of which Kafka owned a translation,[13] the charioteer must control both horses, the nobler and the baser instincts. Here, however, the baser instincts are represented by the groom and the pigsty.

The horses, I believe, suggest "powers stronger than reason or virtue," as Mann called them,[14] human instincts and emotions, and perhaps other superindividual forces as well. No one who has lived an abnormally one-sided life can deal with them; but the groom, being himself instinctual, in however crude a way, can communicate with them. He reminds one of Caliban, and has been equated with the sheer Freudian id[15]—brutal, primitive, and powerful. Having suppressed his own natural emotions, having put them in a pigsty and forgotten them, as it were, the doctor has befouled them and has "fouled himself up" in so doing. One thinks of the fate of Thomas Mann's Aschenbach, who for all his brilliance is a figure related and comparable to Kafka's obscure physician.

The magic speed of the doctor's journey may owe something to Chassidic tales of rabbis who take long trips in horse-drawn carts and arrive in a few minutes.[16] Measurable time plays no part in man's relationship to God.

Section 2. After being welcomed by the boy's parents—they are peasants, apparently—in their stuffy dwelling, the physician finds no symptoms of illness, though the boy's first words are "Doctor, let me die." The protagonist thinks "blasphemously" of the gods (his thoughts of them are sarcastic), then of the groom, of Rose: "How shall I pull her out from under that groom?" Like the groom, the horses are "uncontrollable"; when they poke their heads through the windows, the scene recalls a primitive picture of the Nativity. The doctor "knows" that the boy is healthy, but since he is no "reformer," he will hold his tongue. Overworked and underpaid, he indulges in self-pity. Again he thinks of Rose; if only he can provide for her, he is willing to die. In his situation he must use all possible means merely to keep up with the immediate demands of the day: "I have to take my team out of the pigsty; if they didn't happen to be horses, I'd have to drive with sows." The family cannot understand the situation; the doctor can write prescriptions but cannot communicate with his patients. Twice more he recalls Rose, whom he has now mentioned four times, and admits that he has barely noticed "this lovely girl." Obviously, he is more concerned with her than with the boy. He sees a blood-drenched towel; perhaps after all the patient is really ill.

Interpretation. The airlessness of the room conveys a characteristic sense of oppression, like one of Strindberg's gloomy interiors; the boy's death wish recalls the sibyl quoted by T. S. Eliot: "I wish to die." The thoughts of Rose, whom the physican has neglected for years, recur rhythmically. The doctor's inability to concentrate appears to be pathological. Possibly there is an oblique reference to the Crucifixion in the blood-stained towel, but this does not make the boy a Christ figure.[17]

Section 3. Both the horses neigh; the doctor thinks (sarcastically?) that a "higher court" has arranged the noise to "facilitate" examining the patient. Immediately he sees a large wound near the boy's hip. The word "rose" occurs again, but this time it refers primarily to a color: the wound, open like a surface mine, is infested with "rosy" worms. Yet it is a flower, a lethal flower. Unexpectedly the boy now expresses hope that he will be saved; the family is pleased that the doctor is at last active. He must be the boy's savior, but he is the last man to have the magic power the peasants expect. Now that they have lost their old (Christian) faith, the doctor notes, he is expected "to perform the impossible." He feels old; he thinks again of Rose but does not name her. The doctor is stripped—an especially nightmarish turn of the screw. The onlookers sing:

> Take off his clothes and then he'll heal,
> And if he doesn't, strike him dead!
> It's just a doctor, just a doctor.

When the physician is laid in bed with the boy, the bystanders leave. The boy voices bitter hostility. Yet when he says, "I came into the world with a beautiful wound," he seems to imply that the wound has a beneficial aspect. Carrying the point further, the doctor states consolingly that the wound is a badge of distinction: "Your wound isn't so bad. Made at an acute angle with two strokes of the ax. Many offer their sides and barely hear the ax in the forest, let alone its coming closer to them." When he reassures the boy of this with the words "Take my word of honor as a district doctor along with you over there [*mit herüber*]," he indicates that the boy is dying. The shift of tense back to the past—"And he took it, and became silent"—shows that almost certainly the boy has just died. The doctor thinks desperately of escape; the magic horses are still waiting "faithfully."

Interpretation. As the horses are linked with a "higher court," we may conclude that they are associated with a power which is real but incomprehensible, like the court in *The Trial* or the castle in the novel of that name. Thus while their neighing must have some significance, its occurrence does not prove that the physician is on the right track at that particular moment.[18]

The doctor's failure at once to see the wound implies either that it is a neurotic or metaphysical phenomenon, not a physical one,[19] or that he did not bring himself to face reality on first encountering it, or very probably both. Primarily the wound is the stigma of insight: [20] it is a blessing as well as a curse. "Many offer their sides and barely hear the ax in the forest," we recall. One thinks of the longing for martyrdom, or, in secular terms, of the relation between trauma and creativity propounded by Edmund Wilson in *The Wound and the Bow.* As has been shown, the wound is clearly linked to Rose, and one thinks of a poem Kafka probably never read, William Blake's "The Sick Rose," especially the first two lines:

> O Rose, thou art sick!
> The invisible worm . . . .

Of course the rose is a familiar erotic symbol, as in the *Romance of the Rose* or Goethe's "Heidenröslein." In this context, the wound suggests sex, in its beauty—it is a "flower"—and in the ugliness which Kafka often attributed to it, especially during the time of his two ill-fated engagements to Felice Bauer. "Coitus as a punishment for the happiness of being together," he noted in his diary.[21] The wound seems to link man's basic guilt, or *Urschmerz,* deriving inevitably from self-awareness, to his specifically sexual guilt—as indeed they are linked in Genesis 2–3.

That the doctor is faced with an impossible demand is central to the story as a parable. Like the "man from the country" in "Before the Law" or like Josef K.'s lawyers, he has, by definition, no valid hope. Here, as in "The Penal Colony," Kafka placed his heroes between two worlds, "one dead, the other powerless to be born," where they are faced, in Browning's terms, by "Twenty-nine distinct damnations, / One sure, if another fails." Noting the two meanings of the word *heilen*—"heal" and "save"—Herman Salinger emphasizes that the physician is no savior, and that Kafka did not expect salvation from psychoanalysts [22] (or from any other group, one should add).

When the doctor is put to bed beside the boy, we think of vicarious suffering, of the ordeals imposed on healers as described in *The Golden Bough* [23] and elsewhere. The scene has also suggested to some readers a satire against psychoanalysis.[24] Probably Busacca's observation that the doctor is "in the same bed" with the patient, figuratively as well as literally,[25] is closer to the text. Indeed he is; the awareness of the self-incurred loss of Rose is the doctor's deepest wound: it dooms him but makes him human. Stripping the physician of his clothes makes him literally "naked and afraid." The physician appears as a well-intentioned but rather comic figure: he is able to give the boy some comfort at the end, but his use of his title, "district doctor," reveals bureaucratic pettiness.

Finally we observe that the nightmarish contradictions (in part only seeming contradictions) rise to a crescendo in this scene. The mutual ambivalence in the relationship between the doctor and the boy reminds us of Kafka's obsession with fathers and sons; [26] the doctor is treated both with respect and with contumely; wounds seem normally to be acquired during life, but the boy was born with his. It is also typical of the "dialectical" nature of "A Country Doctor" that our sympathies are divided rather evenly between the physician and the boy.

Section 4. In panic haste the doctor rushes out of the house; he throws his clothes into the carriage, almost losing his fur coat in the process, and swings himself, naked, onto the back of one of the horses. They move slowly this time, the carriage swinging erratically (*irrend*) behind them, the coat dragging in the snow; the command "Lively!" has no effect now. The strange entourage moves "like old men . . . through the desert of snow." For a long time they hear "the new, but erroneous song" sung by the children around the house:

> Rejoice, all ye patients,
> The doctor has been put in bed with you!

The physician knows that he will never get home in this manner; his "blooming" practice has been lost to another, Rose to the groom. Naked in the cold, the "old man" wanders about "with an earthly carriage, unearthly horses." If once one responds to "the false ringing of the night bell," one has been "deceived" and can never make good the mistake.

Interpretation. If we associate the horses with the vitality and emotional health of the doctor, we may infer that he has suffered a drastic breakdown. In any case, this night has radically aged him. That the magic command "Lively!" has no consequences reminds us of his clash with the groom: the actions do not fit his words. Similarly, songs celebrating saviors are "erroneous." Remembering his "blooming" practice seems to lead his mind to Rose. In a mysterious way, the physician knows (or thinks he knows) about his successor. How typical it is of Kafka that this upstart is also frustrated: "for he cannot replace me."

All the worst instincts of man have taken over—"the loathsome groom is raging in my house." It is a glacial period, "the most unhappy of ages": religion has collapsed; science and civilization are powerless. As in Hofmannsthal's *Der Turm,* the most brutal forces are in control. That "rough beast," the groom, is "full of passionate intensity" —to employ Yeats's language in "The Second Coming." Man is not a harmonious organism, but an absurd mixture of disparate "earthly" and "unearthly" elements. To quote one of Kafka's aphorisms: "One of the first signs of dawning insight is the wish to die." [27]

Why does the doctor say that he has been deceived? Precisely because his quite normal reaction to the ringing of the night bell placed him in a situation where he had only an apparent chance of success. He was unsuited by training and temperament to deal with the primal wound of man. His dilemma was really tragic, for if he had not answered the bell, he would have lost all human and professional claim to our respect.

We have then the parable of a man in a situation in which frustration and despair are inevitable—a situation all too familiar to Kafka personally. Perhaps it is not too fanciful to suggest that the imperative to write was Kafka's "night bell," for which he felt impelled to sacrifice his happiness and that of others; yet a man does not really have the freedom to refuse such a summons. Often, at least, Kafka seems to have believed that parables like this reflect the fate, not of some men, but of man as such. The doctor's life at the end is an example of that "durative form of the tragic" [28] which is far harder to bear than is a tragic death. Yet the moment in which the doctor gave the sick boy his "physician's word of honor" did much to vindicate his desperate journey.

4/ Accepting the Universe: Hermann Hesse's *Steppenwolf*

"The value of illness: it gives a man time to acquire the insight that his position, his business, or the society he lives in has made him ill."
—Nietzsche, *Human, All Too Human*

Hesse's *Steppenwolf* (1927) is his most exciting and extreme book, at times deliberately sensational—and it is probably his best. Known as the most romantic of the important German writers of his time, as a continuer of the traditions of Eichendorff and Mörike, Hesse wrote here in a consciously crass, often shocking manner which recalls the cruder aspects of expressionism. The book is an account —among other things—of neurosis, depression, and schizophrenia, in which the hero, Harry Haller (an especially transparent mask for Hermann Hesse), narrowly avoids a complete breakdown. In that sense the story is a flower of evil, though far from evil in itself.

As Ralph Freedman has shown, Hesse tended to write "lyrical" novels, in which poetic expression is far more important than plot or characterization. The lyrical novel—apparently the term is Freedman's own—is especially prevalent in German literature. He mentions *Werther*, Hölderlin's *Hyperion*, and Novalis' *Heinrich von Ofterdingen*, among others.[1]

Accepting Freedman's useful rubric, one can note that by definition lyrical novels tend to be highly autobiographical. This links the type with that characteristically German form of fiction, the *Bildungsroman.* Hesse's more distinguished narratives may be seen as parts of one enormous educational novel. Thus in *Demian,* his first really notable success, we read of the attempts of an adolescent to emancipate himself from a pietistic family, and recall that the *Bildungsroman* grew out of the pietistic tradition in the eighteenth century and often implied a critique of that heritage. In other novels of Hesse's, we read of the hero's struggles to establish himself as a writer or artist, of his loves and marital entanglements, his philosophical flights, his sense of isolation. As in *Wilhelm Meister's Apprenticeship* and its successors, we learn of the cultural experiences, especially the literary ones, which shape his mind.

By the twentieth century, the *Bildungsroman* seemed to be an exhausted form: too many of the most accomplished German novelists had used it; it was associated with romanticism, or the bourgeoisie, or both. Thomas Mann and Hesse were able to revive it only by introducing new approaches and devices—parody, myth, and in Hesse's case Jungian symbolism. Probably the success of his own *Demian* in 1919 and of *The Magic Mountain* five years later encouraged Hesse to employ the form again.

Steppenwolf is an educational novel with a difference. As Egon Schwarz has pointed out, the "Steppenwolf" Harry Haller must undergo a reverse development (*Rück-Bildung*).[2] He is a "man of fifty years"—the title of a novella by Goethe to which Hesse himself alludes [3]—embittered, far from well, with graying hair. Yet like Wilhelm Meister he encounters helpful guides and amiably seductive girls. In his case it is a question of rejuvenation, not of normal growth: he must "die and be born again" or he will be utterly lost; he is closer to Faust than to Wilhelm Meister.[4] Another departure from the usual pattern of the educational novel is that Hesse has provided three narrators. Most of the story consists of the recollections of Harry Haller himself, which he has naturally written down in the first person, but the first chapter is narrated by a former acquaintance who claims to have found these memoirs; he is intelligent and sympathetic to Haller but very bourgeois. The enlightening "Treatise about the Steppenwolf," which comes third, is written "from above," with sarcasm as well as irony, by an anonymous, highly sophisticated author. His diagnosis is so incisive and impersonal that the reader suspects he may be an astute physician or a psychoanalyst.

It soon appears that not only is Haller very sick indeed, but that his sickness is a stigma of insight. Novalis, one of the poets Hesse particularly cherished, has a great deal to say about the positive value of sickness, as does Thomas Mann. In *The Magic Mountain* illness is the mark of European society in the seven years preceding the First World War; Mann's account of life on the mountain is a "time novel" as well as a story of education. *Steppenwolf*, which owes a good bit to Mann,[5] also has this dual aspect. Even the middle-class narrator realizes that Haller's story is a "document of the time":

> For Haller's psychic illness—I realize this now—is not the eccentricity of an individual but the illness of the time itself, the neurosis of his generation, which apparently does not attack only the weak and inferior individuals but precisely the strong, the most intellectual, most gifted [p. 37].

The age is ugly, vulgar, and hypocritical—though the course of the novel makes it clear that it has other, saving aspects which Haller, to his great peril, has scorned or ignored. The contemporary world seems a veritable wasteland. (Appropriately, Eliot quoted Hesse's essay "Looking into Chaos" in the notes to his most famous poem.) Haller is convinced that the respectable forces in society are busily preparing the next war, and is confirmed in this belief when he finds the professor to whom he pays an unfortunate visit sure of the subversive role played by all "Jews and Communists" (p. 92). Further, the Steppenwolf holds that his whole generation is living in an epoch of radical transformation, and that when two cultures intersect, life becomes intensely painful, in fact a hell (pp. 38–39). Kafka's stories "A Country Doctor" and "In the Penal Colony" make the same point.

If *Steppenwolf* is very much part of a tradition, it is at the same time intensely personal. The strong autobiographical element is hardly veiled: Haller's name is only the most obvious of many hints. The style is forthright to the point of ferocity; in this novel Hesse has abandoned the decorum of his earlier books. Yet he has transmuted his experiences into art. Comparison with another of Hesse's works, which records the same experiences in relatively raw form, makes this clear. The verses contained in the volume *Krisis* (1928) are full of images and themes familiar to the reader of *Steppenwolf*, but the difference is enormous. To quote:

> Ich aber saufe und fresse,
> Heisse nicht mehr Hesse,
> Liege bei den jungen Weibern
> Reibe meinen Leib an ihren Leibern,
> Kriege sie satt und drücke ihnen die Gurgel zu,
> Dann kommt der Henker—bringt auch mich zu Ruh.
>
> . . . . .
>
> Bleibe im Nichts und ungeboren . . . .
> Da kann man über alle diese Sachen,
> Lachen, lachen, lachen, lachen.[6]

(But I guzzle and gorge,
Am no longer named Hesse,
Lie with the young females,
Rub my body against theirs,
Get enough of them and choke them to death,
Then comes the hangman and puts me to rest too. . . .
I stay in nothingness, unborn . . . .
Then, about all these things, one can
Laugh, laugh, laugh, laugh.)

These lines could almost be a synopsis of the novel, written by the crudest and most brutal of readers.

It is evidence of Hesse's great talent that he could transform impressions and reactions of this sort into the most challenging of his novels. Perhaps his most striking feat was to make his Harry Haller into a fascinating individual, when he could so easily have been a cliché: another misunderstood intellectual, a "deep," romantically miserable outsider. Largely he accomplished this by viewing Haller—and the whole concept of the "two-souled" rebel—critically, often ironically.

As the novel opens, Haller is obviously on the brink of psychological disaster. He believes that he is half man, half beast; the name Steppenwolf is no mere metaphor to him. Apparently he has lived for many years in a state of controlled schizophrenia; now the disease seems about to get out of control. A specific concern with schizophrenia often is evident in Hesse's work. Beyond that, he was obviously fascinated by duality in general, as the frequent pairs of antithetical characters in his narratives—Sinclair and Demian, Narcissus and Goldmund, and so on—attest. Often the two characters are basically only two aspects of the same person. From the point of view of *Der Steppenwolf*, the possession of two or more "souls" is a sign of complexity as well as a danger. With part of his being, Haller admires and longs for the life of the burgher, like another Tonio Kröger; and very possibly it is this desire for human warmth which enables him to survive.

According to the "Treatise," the Steppenwolf type plays a cardinal role in bourgeois life. It is the half-adjusted, the semioutsiders, who provide vitality and originality for contemporary society, which otherwise would be a mere herd. By an implicit bargain, such half-domesticated wolves are tolerated by the burghers. It is a thoroughly ambivalent relationship, with mixed feelings on both sides.

This compromise, however, does not satisfy Haller. A suicidal type, full of self-hatred, he has long felt the pull of death but has resolved to remain alive until his fiftieth birthday, some two years away at the time the book opens. An oversevere, moralistic education has given him a chronically bad conscience. He is, moreover, one of those who feel with Schopenhauer that individuation is in itself guilt; he longs for "dissolution, back to the Mother, back to God, back to the All" ("Treatise," separately paginated, p. 13). Haller's very heavy drinking seems a deliberate attempt to dull the pain of consciousness in a sort of partial and temporary suicide.

The "Treatise" is most interesting when it becomes a critique of the whole notion of the two-souled man. Real human beings have not two selves but a thousand. Haller comprises not only a wolf, but a "fox, dragon, tiger, ape, and bird of paradise" (T, p. 40). It is up to him to develop all the creative aspects of his being, not to try to "return to nature" or innocence. There is no way back, Hesse proclaims with Schiller, but only a seemingly endless road ahead. "Man" is not something already created but a postulate of the spirit.

Haller, we read, is "enough of a genius to venture the attempt to become a real human being." He is one of the very few who is so qualified, and thus he should no longer live in a world controlled by "common sense, democracy, and middle-class culture" (T, pp. 39–40). (At this point the "Treatise" is extremely Nietzschean; its point of view is more radically aristocratic than that of the novel as a whole.) Haller is called a genius, not because of his earlier writings, which are mentioned only casually, but because of two insights: he sees, however dimly, the goal of becoming human (*Menschwerdung*), and he senses an eternal world of pure form behind the veil of ordinary existence.

What then must the Steppenwolf do to be saved? For the purposes of this novel, it is not a matter of rising to the superhuman heights alluded to in the "Treatise." Rather, to survive at all, he must become human in an earthy, rather humble sense. His education is largely a matter of learning to accept the world, the flesh, and—himself.

Haller learns his lessons largely from "publicans and sinners": he has plunged into the demimonde of a European city of the 1920's, and his companions are the two courtesans Hermine and Maria, and Pablo, a saxophone player. He is also instructed by the figures of Goethe and Mozart, who appear to him in dreams and try to guide him away from morbid obsession with himself. In terms of practical behavior, he must learn not to sulk like a child, not to brood but to find joy in the moment, and above all to laugh. Despite his pietistic upbringing, he learns to enjoy the "garden" of sex without the anxious feeling that he is tasting forbidden fruit. Goethe tells him that the immortals prefer jest to heavy seriousness. Reproached by the Steppenwolf for his untragic view of life,[7] Goethe instances *The Magic Flute* as a serene work of art which is as profound as the tragic works of Kleist or Beethoven. It is a shrewd stroke, for Mozart is not only Haller's favorite artist, but in the novel, his name is a cipher for sheer beauty. Appropriately, it is Mozart who leads Haller to come to terms with the modern world. As a fervent intellectual—and intellectual snob—he has always scorned radio music; Mozart brings him to see that even a crude receiver of the twenties "cannot destroy the essential spirit of such music" (p. 304)—a concerto grosso of Händel's. Haller, in a way, is prepared for such an insight. Early in the book (p. 64), he admitted that the naïve sensuality of American jazz was "honest." Since anti-Americanism is and was so often the stock in trade of certain self-conscious European intellectuals, the admission is significant.

Haller's relations with Goethe and Mozart are very much in the tradition of the *Bildungsroman*. Thus Wilhelm Meister learns from Shakespeare, Keller's Green Henry from Goethe, Mann's Castorp from all and sundry. The basically optimistic point is the same: a man can learn from others not mere facts but insights which may reshape his life.

The climax of Haller's life is the account of his experiences in the section devoted to the Magic Theater; it is, like the "Treatise," one of the two high points of the book. The theme of the theater is announced very early, in the first section of Haller's autobiographical papers. Clearly, it is of major strategic importance. In its own advertising, it is described as "not for everyone. Only for the insane!" (pp. 55–56). Here extraordinary people, crazy or at least crazed, may see the acting out of events, perceive the semblance of reality. It is suggestive that the insane appear both superior and inferior to the average—a view which accords perfectly with the Steppenwolf's (and Hesse's?) feelings of mingled condescension and envy toward the solid citizens.

Also, it must be significant that when Haller does enter the Magic Theater, mirrors are everywhere: he is always seeing himself.

When he ventures into the theater, Haller is in a most exalted state: he has reasons to believe that he will become the lover, and perhaps also the slayer, of Hermine there. (The "love-death" theme is predictably sounded—a regrettably banal touch.) Further, Pablo has just primed him with alcohol and apparently with drugs. This is also a signal to the reader not to interpret Haller's experiences literally. In the theater he is freed of all his inhibitions, finds compensation for all his defeats, acts out all his aggressions. (The psychiatric jargon seems appropriate.) He had to leave the fiction of his "personality" in the checkroom before he entered. Then he takes part in a variety of shows (pp. 251–290); he is in a sort of psychological Coney Island, offering every possible experience. Hesse presents it with great verve. "All the Girls are yours!" one sign proclaims, and the Steppenwolf relives all his erotic experiences. This time each is rewarding.

Another sign runs: "Come to the Merry Hunt! Open Season on Automobiles." In the sideshow Haller can act out his hatred of machines, which as a good European *Kulturpessimist* he loathes, or affects to loathe. The account of Harry and a friend ambushing cars while perched in a tree is wildly comical, comparable to the films *Modern Times* and *A Nous la Liberté*, but more drastic—in fact quite sadistic. Other attractions include a scene devoted to instruction in the Indian art of love (not banal in 1927), another to a presentation of suicide, and a third to one of homosexuality.[8] The most immediately relevant signboard reads: "Guidance for Constructing One's Personality Success Guaranteed." Another, clearly self-mocking, satirizes the "wisdom of the Orient." (Hesse had published *Siddhartha* only a few years before.) The style reaches a feverish height: thus when Mozart appears to him in the theater, he recites a Joycean sort of "pome," beginning "He, mein Junge, beisst dich die Zunge, zwickt dich die Lunge?" (Hey there, young one, what's eating your tongue, or is it your lung?—p. 296). The episode of the theater ends with Haller's symbolic murder of Hermine and the "punishment" which ensues.

It has long been realized that *Steppenwolf* is an account of Hesse's own psychological crisis. It would seem that the Magic Theater is a carefully worked out allegory of psychoanalytic treatment: despite his resistance, the subject is led to relive his past, dramatize his aggressions, and so forth. Here one can destroy automobiles, commit murder, and so on, without sinister consequences. The hoped-for outcome is the one to which the real theater has normally aspired—catharsis; and Haller does seem purged, exhausted, and a bit battered at the end of the "performance."

Haller, to be sure, has not changed so much that he will live the life of an epicure, nor is *Steppenwolf* a eudemonistic book. Rather, the protagonist needs to learn the value of pleasure in order to bring his personality into some sort of balance; otherwise suicide or some other disaster seems certain. Happiness is not his destiny, and he cannot linger indefinitely in the garden of sexuality. Doubtless, life with Maria and Pablo would eventually bore him, but his hedonistic period is one of the numerous metamorphoses he must undergo. Similarly, the end of the book brings no final resolution, any more than a successful psychoanalysis does; but Haller's sense of guilt and dread has been contained and made manageable. Presumably he will no longer find masochistic satisfaction in isolation. Above all, his courage to live has been restored, so that he welcomes being "sentenced" to eternal life: "I was resolved to begin the game once more, once more to taste its torments, to shudder once more at its senselessness, to explore once more and often the hell of my inner self" (p. 313). "I go to encounter for the millionth time the reality of experience," Hesse's fellow exile James Joyce had put it. An earlier Steppenwolf, Nietzsche, phrased it differently; undoubtedly Hesse knew his lines: "Was that life? Very well, then, once more!" [9]

One reason that Haller cannot base his life on the "pleasure principle" lies in his basic *Weltanschauung* (which presumably reflects Hesse's own). While his way of living has been radically changed, this philosophy has remained. Deriving from Schopenhauer (thus ultimately from Buddhism) and Nietzsche, it involves a radical dualism: reality is divided into the realms of time and eternity. Hesse also uses the symbol of the mother (nature) as opposed to the spirit (masculine) or intellect (*Geist*). "Time" contains the tangible world, "reality"; it is equivalent to Schopenhauer's will, and is related to Nietzsche's Dionysiac principle. In other words, its "reality" is ultimately an illusion, but it is nevertheless the very stuff of life. Beyond and above time lies the world of eternity, symbolized by the stars, by classical music, by the immortals, and above all by Goethe and Mozart. It is the realm of disinterested contemplation, aesthetic or intellectual. A few lines from the poem "The Immortals," which just precedes the episode of the Magic Theater, contrast the two realms succinctly:

Immer wieder aus der Erde Tälern
Dampft zu uns empor des Lebens Drang,
Wilde Not, berauschter Ueberschwang,

Blutiger Rauch von tausend Henkersmählern,
Krampf der Lust, Begierde ohne Ende, . . .

Wir dagegen haben uns gefunden
In des Aethers sterndurchglänztem Eis,
Kennen keine Tage, keine Stunden,
Sind nicht Mann noch Weib, nicht jung noch Greis.
Eure Sünden sind und eure Aengste,
Euer Mord und eure geilen Wonnen
Schauspiel uns gleichwie die kreisenden Sonnen [p. 214].

(Ever again, from earth's valleys
The stress of life rises up to us like vapor—
Wild need, drunken excess,
Bloody smoke from a thousand last meals,
Convulsion of lust, desire without end, . . .

But we have found each other
In the icy space of the starry sky;
Know no days, no hours,
Are neither man nor woman, young nor old.
Your sins and your anxieties,
Your murders and your lecherous bliss
Are a spectacle in our eyes, as are the circling suns.)

The sphere of the immortals is as cold as interstellar space. While the "world" is submoral, eternity appears to be supermoral; one can understand that neither Christianity nor democracy would appeal to Haller's "heroic pessimism." Nor can even the most exquisite caresses, the most refined drugs long attract a man who has had glimpses of the eternal.

Since the eternal world is nonmoral, Haller is neither condemned nor forgiven for his offense, the "murder" of Hermine. There is no sort of ethical judgment: men act as they must. But as Haller has broken the rules of the game, confusing appearance with reality, he is "punished": the entire chorus of the immortals laughs at him. Instead of judging him, they announce a diagnosis, in a sardonic but benevolent way.

In arguing that man has not two but a thousand souls, the "Treatise" is very close to Jung's notion of archetypes. (Hesse had been treated, apparently with striking success, by the Jungian analyst Dr. Joseph B. Lang.) [10] Jung gave several different descriptions of the archetype, some of which partially contradict others.[11] The meaning most relevant here is that of a primordial image, found in most or all men: the "Great Mother," the "eternal boy," and the serpent are examples. Since, however, the archetypes are not mere images but shape the personality of a given individual, Hesse can legitimately refer to them as souls. Of course Jung's theories are enormously speculative; they are also often extremely ambiguous.[12] One can see, however, that the theory of archetypes might well appeal to a poet: it is based on the belief that symbols have incalculable psychic power. Jung was a far more appropriate guide for a romantic like Hesse than Freud would have been.

A second Jungian notion, that of the anima or animus, is exploited in *Steppenwolf*. Each man has within him his complementary soul, which appears in the image of woman—his anima; each woman has her complementary animus. The courtesan Hermine, intimately and mysteriously linked to Harry Haller, is indeed his other self, as her name (which of course suggests Hesse's own) implies. Since she is Haller's alter ego, she can also appear masculine and is called Hermann several times; like Goethe's Mignon, she has a hermaphroditic aspect.[13] Toward the end of Haller's symbolic "descent into hell" he kills Hermine (or rather

her image) in a fit of sexual jealousy. Apparently the point is not so much that "each man kills the thing he loves," although it is relevant that killing Hermine is a form of partial suicide; it is rather that a man must "interiorize" his anima; [14] that is, he must come to understand its nature as an image, not an autonomous personality, and thus "overcome" it by dealing with it consciously and rationally. Differently put: we should smile at, not try to destroy, the relics of our "dead selves." Similarly, Pablo may represent a childlike, pleasure-oriented aspect or "soul" of Haller, and Maria is an archetype of the temptress, appealing to sheer sexuality. (Her role corresponds to that of Philine in *Wilhelm Meister*.) Perhaps it is best to see these three figures—Hermine, Pablo, and Maria—in two ways: both as individual characters in the story and as archetypes or "souls" of the Steppenwolf. Thus, in life, if John Smith projects his archetype of the Great Mother upon Betty Jones, she is from a Jungian point of view both herself and an element of his psyche. The technique seems particularly appropriate to the lyrical novel: one "I" speaks through a variety of masks.

The most striking aspect of the form of *Steppenwolf* derives from its use of three narrators; [15] all touch upon many of the same things. In the introduction, the hero's "wolfishness," his suicidal tendency, his illness, and the illness of the age are all presented. Haller's memoirs are naturally much concerned with the same major themes; he comments upon them at length and illustrates them, acts them out, in the course of his narration. Here there is a wealth of incident, episode, and "gallows humor" not found elsewhere in the novel. In his turn, the author of the "Treatise" makes many of the same points as the first narrator, but from a sardonic point of view anticipating that of the immortals. The poem "The Immortals" also restates a central theme of the book.

Thus Hesse relies largely on the technique of repetition and variation, in fact to a degree which suggests a debt to Thomas Mann. The Homeric laughter of the immortals at the end of the novel, for instance, is foreshadowed by the remarks of the "Treatise" on the saving role of humor and by Pablo's affectionately regretful words: "Poor, poor fellow. Look at his eyes! He can't laugh" (p. 165). Leitmotifs are also of great importance; thus the araucaria symbolizes bourgeois life and taste. As Freedman points out, mirror images form a strategic motif throughout the novel, most obviously in the Magic Theater.[16] The "Treatise" is itself a mirror,[17] as is the introduction. Perhaps the most effective and concentrated symbol is that of great music heard over a radio. As the inferior instrument distorts but cannot ruin the music, so time and matter cannot destroy the eternal, and Haller will never survive to view eternity unless he accepts the temporal world—"the radio music of life" (p. 309).

Like many of Gide's works, *Steppenwolf* seems to be intended as a book of liberation and joy. Not that one can imagine Haller as a truly joyful person, but that is the direction of the book. To restate its themes at length would be to trivialize them; taken out of the fabric of the novel, they seem banal. To recapitulate briefly: the Steppenwolf comes to realize that he must love himself as well as his neighbor; he is freed, at least partially, from the sense of guilt; he comes to cherish the surface as well as the depths. Yet we sense that it will be a very long time before he learns to laugh. Steppenwolf is a Nietzschean type, striving toward a health he will hardly attain, a martyr of heroic pessimism rather than a superman. Much of the appeal of the book lies in this paradoxical tension. The novel is a deliberately dissonant hymn to joy.

5/ Myth versus Secularism: Religion in Thomas Mann's *Joseph*

"'I am the Lord thy God,' Moses said, at the risk that they would really think he was."
—Thomas Mann, *The Tables of the Law*

When Thomas Mann chose a biblical subject as the theme of a major work, he exposed himself to legitimate questions about his own religious point of view. Had he abandoned the attitude of such earlier novels as *Buddenbrooks*, in which the Christian figures are at best pathetic, or of *The Magic Mountain*, where the only avowed Christian is the basically unpleasant Naphta? Such questions are relevant in Mann's case; for except in a few stories and such relatively minor books as *The Transposed Heads* and *The Holy Sinner*, he was never a practitioner of *l'art pour l'art*. Even *Felix Krull* implies a moral standpoint, a *Weltanschauung*. Various critics have attempted to describe Mann's religious attitude: Anna Hellersberg-Wendriner, for instance, senses a "mystique of distance from God" ("Mystik der Gottesferne") in his work.[1] Ronald Gray has maintained that Mann really has no religious or ethical orientation; his whole attitude, Gray believes, shows his ambivalence or his nihilism, or both.[2] Although Mann himself, like many other humanists, moved toward a united front with Christianity during the Nazi period, he claimed even then to be endowed with no more than an undogmatic religiosity.

In a sense it is paradoxical that Mann worked with religious (or quasi-religious) materials in the twenties and thirties, in decades when he was particularly fascinated by the ideas of Sigmund Freud. Freud, after all, considered religion an illusion and maintained in one of his last works that Moses was an Egyptian. Intrigued and impressed though he was by the importance of myth as a key to the unconscious and to primitive thought, Freud utterly rejected a mythical approach in dealing with contemporary affairs and personal matters. In a most friendly letter to Mann on the occasion of the novelist's sixtieth birthday, he extended no congratulations, for, he stated, "the bestowal of wishes is trivial and seems to me a regression to an era when mankind believed in the magic omnipotence of thought." [3] This seems unduly austere, but it makes Freud's own position completely clear: to think mythically in the twentieth century would be neurotic.

On some levels, the reasons for Mann's evocation of the world of the Old Testament are clear enough. We know that he planned, around 1926, to write an introduction to a book of illustrations of the Joseph story, and that he was intrigued by Goethe's remark in *Dichtung und Wahrheit:* "This artless tale is most charming; only it seems too long; one feels called on to work it out in detail." [4] Above all, Mann wished to break a lance for the Jews, the people who primarily represented *Geist* to him, in a time seething with anti-intellectualism and racial hatred. A shibboleth of the pseudo romanticists of those days was myth, interpreted to make the term refer to the opposite of civilized thinking. Myth, then was a major weapon of reaction disguised as progress.[5] Mann believed, however, that genuine romanticism implies faith in the future.[6] Characteristically, he decided to rescue the myth from the Fascists and proto-

Fascists. In his *Joseph and His Brothers* he created a humane myth, a symbolic story of the upward development of man and his concept of God. As the tetralogy proceeds, however, its thrust from the mythic dimness of the patriarchal world to the clear light of Joseph's realm becomes increasingly evident. Perhaps this thrust from myth toward reason may also be read as a transition from theism to secularism.

Before taking up the religious and mythical aspects of the Joseph novels, however, I should quickly note that they have other important facets—political, social, autobiographical, and of course formal. Perhaps the comic element is as important as any other. In a highly suggestive, beautifully written essay, Mark Van Doren has considered *Joseph* as a comedy in four parts. Van Doren notes its brilliant conversation, its relaxed, leisurely handling of time, and Joseph's failure, despite all his preternatural intelligence, really to understand himself and his own limitations.[7] Mann's skepticism is interpreted as a concomitant of his universality:

> The genius of Mann is skeptical in the finest sense of an often misapprehended term. It was not that he believed nothing: he believed everything; he liked ideas, and could live with all of them at once. No sooner did one start up in his brain than another came to reinforce, illuminate, or check it. This was why he could turn so soon from tenderness to pathos, and why he could mock the very man he loved the most. These transformations of his mood will bewilder anyone who does not comprehend how serious at last the comic spirit is. Nothing in man is more serious than his sense of humor; it is the sign that he wants all the truth, and sees more sides of it than can be soberly and systematically stated; it is the sign, furthermore, that he can remember one idea even while he en-

tertains another, and that he can live with contradiction. It is the reason at any rate that we cannot take seriously one whose mind and heart have never been known to smile. The gods do not weep; they smile. Eternity is something like the sun.[8]

First of all, I should like to examine the introductory chapter of *Joseph*, "Descent into Hell." (It is typical of the benign irony of the work that there is nothing infernal about this descent.) As has been noted, "Descent into Hell" serves as a quasi-musical overture to the tetralogy. Opening with the magnificent statement "Deep is the well of the past," it also functions as an introduction to the depths of time and to the mythical mode of thinking. Of at least equal importance in the interpretation of the novel are the few pages devoted to retelling the Gnostic myth of the fall of the soul.[9] In Mann's adaptation, the soul—"*die* Seele"—became enamored of sheer, unformed matter; God then created the world of forms so that "she"[10] might mingle with matter and thus form living men. In her infatuation, she forgot her divine origin. To redeem the soul, God sent a messenger, the spirit—"*der* Geist"—Logos; his mission was to destroy the physical world. Both life and death would then cease to exist, and the soul, free of her earthly entanglements, would return to heaven like a prodigal daughter returning to her true home. The spirit, however, actually did fall in love with the soul, despite or because of the fact that she had been interfused with the material element. Both literally and morally, the spirit and the soul had fallen; they were, or seemed to be, alienated from God.

From this myth—which of course has striking analogies with the account of the Fall as related in Genesis—Mann boldly infers that man is older than the material world.[11]

Spirit and soul,[12] in their involvement with matter, must be images of man, that two-souled, problematic creature who is irresistibly attracted by both the sensuous and the divine. Yet God deeply loves man, is fascinated by his dual nature, and finds him far more interesting than those representatives of pure spirit, the angels. (Naturally enough, the angels—who refer to man sarcastically as "the angel-beast"—bitterly resent this, as does a recent commentator.)[13]

To press the argument a step further, I suggest that this myth, the "romance of the soul," mirrors the action of the novel as a whole, just as "The Lamentation of Dr. Faustus" is a mirror and symbol of *Doctor Faustus*, and as "Before the Law" is a miniature recapitulation of Kafka's *The Trial*. As I shall try to show, the spirit in Mann's myth plays a role analogous to Joseph's own. Mann wittily compares the spirit's romance with the soul to the case of an ambassador who becomes so entranced with another nation that he betrays his own:

> As it often occurs that the ambassador of one realm, if he is long stationed in another, hostile land, is ruined from the point of view of his own country. For he comes to feel so much at home . . . that he gradually becomes unfit to represent the interests of his own nation and has to be recalled. This or something like it happens to the spirit in the course of its mission.[14]

Similarly, Joseph's role as the mediator between Pharaoh and the people suggests the spirit's mediation between God and matter; as "metatron" or second in command in his realm, Joseph also recalls the Gnostic demiurge. Like the spirit, he leaves his home for a lower realm—to his father, Egypt is a sort of hell—and lingers indefinitely in a world which attracts him sensually and intellectually. Even in the

Bible, we remember, Joseph remained in Egypt and was buried there.[15] Again like the spirit, however, he is not deprived of his higher nature, nor does he forget his native land. And Egypt is by no means a hell, any more than the world in Mann's very anti-Gnostic variation of the myth is really evil. God can never have seriously intended to destroy it.[16] Mann's interpretation of the "romance of the soul" reminds one of Robert Frost's lines:

> But God's own descent
> Into flesh was meant
> As a demonstration
> That the supreme merit
> Lay in risking spirit
> In substantiation.[17]

In character as well as role, Joseph reminds us of the spirit. A mixture of savior and rogue, he reflects spirit fused with ensouled matter. He is *tâm*—a combination of "Yes" and "Yes-No." [18] The "lower" aspects of his blessing, the biblical "blessings . . . of the womb," link him to the flesh and the senses. Joseph's wittiness is one of his major attractions, and wit itself is a messenger, the "mediator between the paternal and maternal inheritances," reconciling the principles of light and dark.[19] (Wit is conceived in the novel largely in its older meaning of skill in forming ingenious intellectual combinations.)

Actually, his secular, humanistic endowment is closer to Mann's taste than is the purely spiritual blessing which Judah finally receives. Similarly, as we have seen, Mann's God prefers men to angels. His God is as genial and tolerant as is the God of the "Prologue in Heaven" in *Faust*, a deity wittily compared to Old King Cole by the protagonist of Santayana's *The Last Puritan*. Indeed, the angels believe that God has a less serious attitude toward the moral realm that does the fallen angel Semael, the Mephistophelean but hardly satanic champion of evil; [20] and these jealous servants of God even hint that he himself contains an element of evil: [21] in other words, he is *tâm*.

In evoking the world of Jacob and his ancestors, Mann took great pains to elucidate the mythical way of thought. He explains elaborately how "moon grammar" reduces the three modes of time to an eternal present, and how patriarchal figures identify themselves with their archetypical predecessors. Napoleon's identification of himself with Julius Caesar and Seneca's line "Medea nunc sum!" are examples of this sort of mythical thinking, which still occasionally persists. Mann's own sense of *unio mystica* with Goethe, and Hitler's apparent obsession with Wagnerian heroes are twentieth-century examples. As the long novel proceeds, however, "moon grammar" is increasingly replaced by the clear light of day. Once he has matured, Joseph thinks and acts realistically and logically. Freud would have approved.

Moreover, various antimythical forces operate throughout the tetralogy. Characters are psychologically analyzed and "unmasked" with a subtlety which owes much to Nietzsche and Freud. Thus Isaac becomes blind *so that* he can give the blessing to Jacob rather than to Esau, and Joseph seems to have an unconscious drive to anger his brothers. There is a wealth of realistic detail, recalling Mann's statement: "We can't do without realism. It is the backbone, the element which convinces." [22] Occasional flashes of irony or parody distance us from the realm of myth: the scene in an Egyptian border fortress recalls a modern customs and immigration inspection; Egyptian nationalism suggests German chauvinism. It is even said that God has "a great theological career" before him. In the fourth volume, Joseph's sense of acting out a story planned long before by God becomes increasingly obvious. At the end, the fairy-tale note provides a culminating *Verfremdungseffekt:*

> And so ends the lovely story
> and divine invention of
> *Joseph and His Brothers.*

What a myth, but alas, only a myth! (to paraphrase Faust's exclamation).

The reciprocal relation between Abraham and God is complex and subtle. On the one hand, Abraham has no doubt that God objectively exists; on the other, he realizes that he is himself "to a certain extent God's father." God needs Abraham and the other prophets to help Him develop from a crude tribal divinity to a genuinely monotheistic deity. The narrator neither affirms nor denies God's objective reality, but possibly *The Tables of the Law*, a pendant to *Joseph*, affords insight into Mann's attitude.[23]

Paradoxically, the tetralogy's very wealth and richness of mythological reference have a relativizing effect. That Joseph's life reflects the myths of Osiris, Adonis, Dionysus, and other gods, and that it anticipates the Crucifixion and Resurrection of Jesus Christ may suggest that all such accounts are only mythically or symbolically true. If the mysterious messengers who frequently appear throughout the novel are mythically both angels and the god Hermes, perhaps *de facto* they are neither. And it is by no means clear that Pharaoh Ikhnaton's monotheism is inferior to Hebrew religious concepts.

Since *The Tables of the Law* was written immediately after the completion of *Joseph* (in 1943) and plays in the same Hebrew and Egyptian milieu, one may turn to it for additional illumination of the novel. Since Mann characterized it as on the whole an "insignificant improvisation,"[24] one should not overemphasize its importance; but precisely because it is a not too seriously intended work of art, Mann felt himself free, I believe, to express his personal opinions. Here mythical thinking is not practiced; the author is much more outside—and above—the story. Aside from its immediate function as propaganda against the Nazis, the tale is interesting largely in its concept of God and its portrait of Moses as the artist; the two elements are closely interrelated.

Moses is seen as a sculptor of human beings: he molds the Hebrew people, who have become crude and demoralized in their long Egyptian captivity. By providing the erring nation with a code of moral and practical behavior, he instills conscience into it. Later, after inventing the Hebrew alphabet, he hews out the Decalogue in stone twice, illuminating the letters with his own blood. (The Bible states expressly that the Commandments were written by God's finger.)[25] Half an Egyptian,[26] he has the necessary artistic distance from his human raw material. He is passionate and sensual, but, as in Judah's case, his very passions make him "hunger and thirst after righteousness." Moses' greatest creation however is not the Decalogue or the molding of the Jewish people but—God.

Such an interpretation may seem startling or worse, but it is in line with the skeptical, downright Voltairean tone of the work. All the miracles are rationalistically explained; the Hebrews behave at least as badly as the Egyptians; and Moses, soon to be the transcriber (or author) of the commandment forbidding adultery, has a lush Moorish concubine, since his wife no longer appeals to his senses. In fact, "God" (Moses' conscience or unconscious?) never forbids anything Moses really wants. In recounting Moses' proscription of incest, Mann includes the outrageous, or outrageously amusing, clause: "Thou shalt not sleep even with thine aunt." [27]

Revealingly, Moses often links himself most intimately with God: he tells the people that "Jehovah and I" want them to behave decently.[28] Other turns of phrase are even more significant. When Moses castigates the mob for attributing salvation to the golden calf (in *The Tables of the Law* it is a sexual symbol, a golden bull), he states that he alone led the people out of Egypt—adding the formula "saith the Lord" [29] as an afterthought. The following sentence is the most explicit of all: " 'I am the Lord thy God,' he said, at the risk that they would really think he was." [30] In forbidding false witness, he employs the threat "I will devour him"; [31] later, after the affair of the golden calf, God threatens to devour the whole nation of backsliding Hebrews.[32]

Res ipsa loquitur: "God" is a projection of Moses' own imperious will. Yet Moses is by no means a hypocrite; rather, he has, like all Mann's artists, an "all too human" side. Nor is Mann nihilistic or basically cynical here: he upholds the Decalogue and the symbolic validity of God, though only at the cost of sacrificing God's actuality. "God" knows that men will not keep the Commandments; "God"-Moses knows all too well that he has broken at least two of them himself. But Moses has learned the hard way that violation of the moral code imbues the sinner with an "ice-cold" sense of anxiety and guilt—"and it were better for him if he had never been born." [33]

To return to *Joseph:* we recall that it traces God's development and "great theological career"; it is in that sense, as in others, a *Bildungsroman.* But educational novels end, and whatever has developed will presumably decline. We note also that Joseph himself is really far closer to Hermes than to Jehovah; and Hermes is of course only a charming symbol. Yet *Joseph* is not a "debunking," antimythical novel. As Käte Hamburger well says, "The story of Joseph is only an indication, a step toward and a weak reflection of the divine myth; but it *is* after all an indication, a step, a reflection." [34]

While Thomas Mann believed—symbolically—in many gods, he believed in them only to the extent that they represented to him a humane, rational ethic and view of the world. To him, intellect and wit were essential parts of humanity; as Aristotle said, a stupid person cannot be good. That Mann preferred Erasmus to Luther is relevant here. Mann was far too conciliatory and too courteous to proclaim shrilly that "God is dead"; his God is a construction, a projection of the best in man, a beneficent fiction. He writes in *Joseph* of a God of the future, but he may well have envisioned a future without God. Here a quotation from Harvey Cox is very relevant to an "urban-secular" writer like Mann:

> The central question is: What are the sources of meaning and value by which man lives his life? Are they created and imposed by God, or does man invent them himself? It is characteristic of urban-secular man that he perceives himself as the source of whatever significance the human enterprise holds. His perception is confirmed by modern cultural anthropology and by the sociology of knowledge. Symbol systems, the constellations of meaning by which human life is given value and direction, are seen as projections of a given society. They change when the society changes and in predictable ways. There is nothing timeless or divine about them.
>
> But does not this theory of the source of meaning in human life rob God of His divine prerogative? How can we accept

this grandiose assessment of man's place in the universe without at the same time limiting or degrading God? [35]

How indeed? Mr. Cox never really answers his own rhetorical question; far more than Mann he wants to have the best of both worlds, avant-garde and theological. Not at all cynically, Mann implies that "an honest God's the noblest work of man." Many may find this frivolous, but Mann gave in *Joseph* his aspect of truth—next to love the highest of our values. As Peter Gay notes in his splendid vindication of the Enlightenment: "In their more pacific, generous moods, the *philosophes* conceded to the pious man his share of honesty, but they considered him incapable of pursuing an inquiry to its end—the man caught in myth must make the myth, not the truth, his final value." [36] If I understand Mr. Gay correctly, he implies that myth and symbol have great value, but that a man must decide whether or not they should prevail over rational truth: he *cannot* have it both ways. The kingdom evoked in *Joseph* is secular, a kingdom of man at his best, in which human beings err, as in *Faust*, but in which human adventurousness, inventiveness, and above all, human love are decisive. *Joseph* is a statement of a paradoxical faith in man, doubly paradoxical when one thinks of the dark times in which it was written.

6/ Vitality and Tradition: Two Novels by Heimito von Doderer

"Denn der Boden zeugt sie wieder,
Wie er sie von je gezeugt."

("For the earth breeds them again
As it has always bred them.")
—Goethe, *Faust II*

Die Strudlhofstiege ("The Strudlhof Stairway")

In the rather barren state of German and Austrian literature immediately after the war, the appearance of so vigorous and original a work as Heimito von Doderer's *Die Strudlhofstiege*[1] was a reassuring event. While Doderer was by no means a "new" writer—his "Byways and Landscapes," a collection of verse, appeared in 1923, and his first novel, "The Breach," in 1924—it was not until 1951, when *Die Strudlhofstiege* was published, that he achieved a work of major scope. In this long novel of Viennese life Doderer displays a formidable range of talents: the gift of creating a number of "felt," convincing characters, sensuosity and exuberance of language, and the ability to arrange complicated lines of plot in a controlled pattern. The book is not without its lapses and *longueurs*, but it leaves one with the impression of vitality and richness—qualities not too common in any literature.

Die Strudlhofstiege is not easy to place or to describe. While it is set mainly in twentieth-century Vienna, with the events clustering around the two focal dates of 1911 and 1925, it is not primarily a social novel, nor, in the usual sense of the term, a *Zeitroman*. J.-F. Angelloz' use of the term "comédie humaine" [2] seems apt. Political happenings are rarely, though shrewdly, commented on; [3] the Church is barely mentioned; there is no attempt to represent all the classes or important groups of Viennese society. It is character that concerns Doderer primarily; the plot, ingenious and complex though it is, is chiefly a device for examining personalities and their interrelations. The theme of education through living is important, particularly in the lives of Lieutenant (later Major) Melzer, the admirable if somewhat commonplace hero of the novel, and the more problematic coprotagonist, René von Stangeler; but *Die Strudlhofstiege* is only in part a *Bildungsroman*. And while the decline of the Austro-Hungarian Empire inevitably plays some part, this is not a story of decadence; in fact, it is surprisingly optimistic and at times almost too *gemütlich*.[4]

The key to the novel lies in the title. The handsome Strudlhofstiege, built in 1910 by Johann Theodor Jäger, leads down from the aristocratic quarter around the Boltzmanngasse to the more bourgeois regions of the Alsergrund. In the novel it links the two social and intellectual levels figuratively as well as literally. Moreover, Doderer uses the stairway with its ascending ramps [5] as a stage, in two different senses. It serves as a theater for his characters: at the first great crisis, he contrives to group his figures there as artfully as a modern director might deploy the actors on a *Jessnertreppe*. One is reminded of the famous scene in *Tom Jones* where Fielding manages to bring his characters to the inn together. Stangeler thinks of the stairway as a "stage" of life, a *Theatrum Mundi*. In his groping way, Melzer senses that it somehow symbolizes his own existence:

Even though he did not see exactly a stage of life in these rising stairs and gently rising ramps . . . , Melzer was somehow stirred here to an awareness of the depth of his own existence, however modest and insignificant that may have been [p. 330].

Indeed, the stairway has a strong attraction for the people who live near it, whether on the higher or the lower level; it seems to be the home of a beneficent *genius loci.* Finally, it becomes a symbol of Vienna itself: "The master of the stairs has selected one bit of our multitudinous lives in the metropolis and showed us what dignity and decorum are to be found everywhere in it" (p. 331). It might be said to represent the continuing and reinvigorating power of Viennese tradition, a centripetal force holding a society together.

In the subtitle, the words "die Tiefe der Jahre"—the depth of the years—contain another important clue to the author's intention. As has been noted, the actions take place during two different periods, separated by about fourteen years; and Doderer shifts between the two planes of time just as he alternates between two social and geographical levels. The main characters in the events of 1910–1911 also take leading parts in those of 1923–1925; the author gives some brief indication of their fate during the intervening years. The skillful use of this device enables Doderer to give his personages the dimension of time, and hence a heightened degree of reality. He is most notably successful with René von Stangeler, almost the only intellectual in the book, and incidentally an autobiographical figure.[6] Stangeler undergoes only partially the typical upward development of the hero of the *Bildungsroman;* in this self-portrait the optimism inherent in the genre, and in this novel in particular, is muted. His *Bildung* is the more impressive for the skepticism and restraint with which it is represented.

"Depth of the years" implies much more than the effects of the passage of time. It seems to refer above all to memory, to a way of living in awareness of one's own past which is in itself a "deepening" experience. Doderer's characters are anything but philosophical recluses, yet recollection is an integral part, one might almost say an institution, in the lives of several of them. More than once, the lower levels of the mind are compared to the depths of the sea; not all that has sunk into the unconscious can be retrieved, but at least, bubbles will rise to the surface. Any comparison with Proust must be most cautiously made. Quite apart from questions of literary rank, the two writers are radically different in many ways. Doderer was bold enough, in the course of a lecture in Paris, to speak of the "powerful dynamics of boredom" in Proust's work.[7] Yet there are certain affinities, and Doderer may have learned something from *A la recherche du temps perdu.*

The plot is too complicated to recount in any detail, dealing as it does with the fortunes of some twenty persons, each of whom is presented rather fully, a few very extensively. A closely interrelated group of members of the Viennese upper middle class—the Stangelers, Melzer, the Pastrés, Mary K., and their lovers, friends, and acquaintances—appear in the first part of the novel as young people. Through René von Stangeler's friendship with Paula Schachl, a girl of rather humble background, a connection is established with the more modest world of the region at the foot of the Strudlhofstiege. This "lower" world is by no means treated patronizingly, but appears in an idyllic and somewhat sentimental glow: Doderer regards the petty-bourgeois milieu with particular affection. The prewar action reaches its climax in a scene of mean and most unpleasant betrayal, which serves to catalyze the action, separating the men of good will from the lukewarm and the evil. In the postwar action, the same major figures, and some others, are again drawn closely together. A second betrayal, planned by Editha Pastré, who had engineered the first one, is frustrated at the last moment. Certain leading figures are now able, thanks to matured insight, to correct, as it were, the mistakes committed fourteen years before. Thus Melzer, who had been too callow and inhibited to accept love, finally achieves it; he also makes atonement, at a dramatic moment, for the injury he had inflicted. The two "heroes," Melzer and Stangeler, educate each other, to a large extent. Melzer is a modern Parsifal who has failed to ask the right question; Stangeler, less "pure," is a Gawain of the intellect.

Like a good comedy, the novel reaches its happy ending in a marriage; in fact, even Editha Pastré, the one really evil person in the whole work, is forgiven and will presumably sin no more. Yet on reading and rereading the book, one is convinced that there is a great deal more to it than any plot synopsis could suggest, that while the action may be at times sensational, at times banal, the work has its beauties and its serious values.

The greatest originality of *Die Strudlhofstiege* lies in the style. It is rich, varied, at times heavily ornamented—it has been loosely called baroque—at times downright colloquial; levels of language are deliberately mixed. English, French, and Latin phrases appear freely; puns and conceits abound; some of them are admirable, some outrageous. Doderer is anything but a purist; he seems to rejoice in the possibilities of a sort of New High Austrian which has taken its vocabulary and idioms from the most varied sources, and to be determined to exploit every one of them. What might be called, *mutatis mutandis*, the Joycean strain in Doderer reaches its climax in the language of a highly eccentric retired Prussian cavalry officer, one of the very few Germans in the novel, who is known simply as Der Rittmeister:

Na warte mal. . . . Da geht einem der Hut hoch. Duplizitäts-Gören. Scheich ül Islam. Da kann ma nur mehr 'n bemoostes Haupt beuteln. Sunt certi denique fines. . . . War natürlich vorher hier. Irish banc. Na warte mal, dich lass' ich springen. Aber gemach, gemach. Später, peut-être. Für heutabend woll' ma's noch verknusen! Das ist der Fluch der bösen Tat, dass sie fortzeugend Übles mus gebären. Oller Jambenfritze. Ω πρὸς Θεῶν. (oh, bei den Göttern!) In die Zirkel geritten! So 'n Gaul. Springt auf der falschen Hand ein. Ihr könnt mich [pp. 632–633].

(Now just wait. . . . That's the last straw. Double-dealing girls. Sheik of Islam. A man can only shake his hoary head. Sunt certe denique fines. . . . [Surely, there are limits, finally.] She was here before, naturally. Irish bank. Well wait, I'll fix your goose. But gently, gently. Later, *peut-être*. For this evening we'll put up with it. That is the curse of wicked act, that it must breed and bear more evil deeds. Old iambic Fritz [Schiller]. Ω πρὸς Θεῶν. [Oh, by the gods!] Ride around the ring. What a horse. Jumps the wrong way. You can kiss my . . . .)

The conversational style of the Rittmeister (who is occasionally referred to as the *Zerrüttmeister*—the master of disorder) reads like a parody of Doderer's own comic manner. That Doderer pays eloquent tribute in this novel to the ordered clarity of Roman prose comes as a bit of a surprise; but like his Rittmeister, he has obviously had a humanistic education. Elsewhere, as in his symbolic novella *Das Letzte*

Abenteuer ("The Last Adventure"), his style can be almost classic.

The usual mode of narration in *Die Strudlhofstiege* is relaxed, chatty, parenthetical, and highly digressive, though at moments of tension Doderer can write simple, hard-hitting narrative prose; he varies his *tempi* admirably. Generally he uses a style which demands close attention from the reader, full of associative transitions and of allusions to images, events, or leitmotifs which have gone before. The action may shift rapidly from one of the many major figures to another; and from time to time the reader is moved some fourteen years forward—or backward—without any explicit warning. On first reading, the novel can be confusing, but the author does not make unfair use of his stratagems. This is not really a "difficult" book, but it is densely packed and must be taken slowly.

In a novel so concerned with time, one might expect that the leitmotifs would owe something to Mann's, but actually they are closer to Fontane's: they seem to aim more at humorous characterization than at musicality or the recapture of the past. Thus a somewhat crusty official of the old school is fond of saying, "Basically all that is dirty business"; the vagaries of the retired officer regularly evoke the comment "That's the Captain for you"; and we are repeatedly told of Major Melzer's very gradual progress toward the acquisition of "ordinary common sense" (*Zivilverstand*). Perhaps one should speak of comic repetitions, as in Lessing, rather than leitmotifs. Indeed, the novel is, broadly speaking, a comic one, despite some gruesome and harrowing incidents; but as in so many Austrian comedies, from Ferdinand Raimund's to Hofmannsthal's, a serious intention lies beneath the surface.

Not the least of Doderer's gifts is his delicate, at times almost lyric sensibility. This appears most clearly in his recording of sense impressions: the odor of damp asphalt after rain, the croaking of frogs rising like a singing column of sound ("eine singende Säule im Gehör"),[8] the "filtered" reddish light of evening, the subaqueous tone of the light under densely leaved trees. The "feel" of a landscape is always sharply rendered, whether it is a small ravine near Vienna, the mountains of the Semmering, or a forest in Hungary. His metaphors are striking, at times bizarre, and as one would expect in this book, often humorous. Thus Melzer, while still withdrawn in bachelorhood, is seen as a crab, half-hidden in the mud at the bottom of a stream.

Another favorite metaphor illuminates Doderer's psychology. He is fond of comparing the human mind to a system of tracks, a *Bahnnetz;* as the thoughts move in periods of reflection, they are "switched" from one line to another. Similarly, he refers often to the "tropoi," the habitual turning points, of the psyche. His more perceptive characters repeatedly engage in periods of combined recollection and thought, renewing the past to illuminate the present. Doderer would seem to be convinced as Franz Grillparzer of the necessity of *Sammlung*—concentration—but is much more sanguine than the dramatist about the possibility of its achievement.

Keenness of psychological and moral awareness is one of Doderer's particular talents. His motivation may seem arbitrary but is actually careful and subtle. Thus Mary K.'s mutilation in a traffic accident is no gratuitous horror: Doderer shows in detail her distraught state of mind before the disaster. However much one may distrust a geographical approach to literature, it seems reasonable to relate these insights into the complexities of life to the Viennese tradition. Doderer's many *aperçus* are less skeptical than Schnitzler's, less mordant than Musil's or Karl Kraus's, but the best of them are equally penetrating. Thus he comments on the effect of unrealized potentialities: "Every buried talent sends up a small pestilence to the surface of the soul" (p. 147); and he has René Stangeler remark that there should be two separate dictionaries, and eventually separate languages, for the two sexes. "A person in love would have to learn the other language, instead of perverting his own" (p. 498). More seriously, another character in the novel indicates the effect of one's role in life on the "private" personality: "No one can turn over all his external life [*das äussere Leben*] to a mask, and remain behind it in self-sufficient integrity. With such a chasm, the bridge of reality, which connects the inner and the outer, would collapse" (p. 273).

Elsewhere, Doderer goes beyond this position and affirms one of his most characteristic beliefs, the essential identity of the exterior and interior worlds. To distinguish instinctively, at all times, between appearance and reality would be in his view a mark of profound corruption; and Stangeler, who often seems to speak for his author, declares that he does not believe in any real difference. Doderer quotes the proposition of the fourteenth-century Church council, "Anima forma corporis," and translates: "Die Seele gliedert den Leib" (The soul organizes the body—p. 361). In fact, he seems to go beyond this and suggest an affinity between the personality of his characters and the beloved Viennese and Austrian landscapes; but he is never heavy-footed enough to assert such a claim directly. This romantic assumption—if indeed it is present—is at most tentatively implied.

Generally, Doderer moves on a less abstract plane. He seems primarily interested in individuals, whom he regards, in this book at least, with tolerance and usually with affection. Evil, as portrayed in Editha Pastré, appears trivial and rather stupid. His point of view is as tolerant, as humane ("mänschlich") as that of Clawdia Chauchat, but he has two serious moral concerns—the problems of maturing and of communication—and these are so closely linked as to appear as two aspects of the same happy state of achieved humanity. Thus Melzer must shed his crablike shell before he can become "a simple human being, the hardest thing to be that there is." (Similarly the protagonist of Doderer's light novel *Die erleuchteten Fenster*—"The Lighted Windows" —must break the "little sac" which envelops him before he can become a real person.) René Stangeler is "blind," though eventually he attains at least partial vision. An intellectual, he has a certain tendency toward half measures and indecision. Both of these protagonists realize their maturity only when they are able to make lasting commitments to others. As in Hofmannsthal, marriage is the great bridge leading from isolation into the "real" world.

It is strange indeed that Angelloz speaks of the "pessimisme inquiétant" of the book.[9] His reference to Doderer as a "romancier . . . de le décadence" would be more defensible if he were referring to certain of the earlier works; for the positive and genial attitude of *Die Strudlhofstiege* represents only one of the author's modes. In earlier novels, like *Ein Mord, den Jeder Begeht* (*Every Man a Murderer*, 1938) and *Ein Unweg* ("A Detour," 1941), the tone is very different. The mood of Doderer's second major novel, *Die Dämonen* (*The Demons*, 1956), which pictures the decay of the first Austrian republic, is in part apocalyptic. Even in *Die Strudlhofstiege*, hideous things occur, like the suicide of Etelka Stangeler and the accident which befalls the admirable Mary K. In this book, as elsewhere, Doderer shows a tendency toward sensationalism, and at times toward a mystification reminiscent of the detective story. As if to remind us that *Gemütlichkeit* is not his supreme value, he prefaces his comic novel with verses whose tone is by no means in harmony with the narrative that follows:

"Auf die Strudlhofstiege zu Wien"

Wenn die Blätter auf den Stufen liegen
herbstlich atmet aus den alten Stiegen
was vor Zeiten über sie gegangen.
Mond darin sich zweie dicht umfangen
hielten, leichte Schuh und schwere Tritte,
die bemooste Vase in der Mitte
überdauert Jahre zwischen Kriegen.

Viel ist hingesunken uns zur Trauer
und das Schöne zeigt die kleinste Dauer.

("To the Strudlhof Stairway in Vienna"

When the leaves lie on the steps
there rises from the old stairs, like the breath of autumn,
that which passed over them long ago.
Moon in which two held each other close,
light shoes and heavy tread;
the moss-covered vase in the center
outlasts the years between the wars.

Much has sunk in ruins and we grieve:
the beautiful is the least enduring.)

Doderer's work combines several different strains. Certain of the earlier novels, like *Every Man a Murderer*, recall Jacob Wassermann and perhaps Dostoevsky; here, as Lennartz notes, he shows affinities to Jean Paul and Raabe.[10] A reader of English literature is occasionally reminded of Dickens. *Die Strudlhofstiege* is not fully representative of Doderer. For all its richness, it is not his most sustained work of art. Yet it reveals the author as a master of the comic use of language, fresh, bold, and extraordinarily rich in invention.

"The Waterfalls of Slunj"

Doderer's death on December 23, 1966, deprived us of a fascinating writer, a novelist whose importance is by no means limited to Austrian literature. At seventy, Doderer seemed to have lost none of his vigor: his "Novel Number 7," planned as a tetralogy, was perhaps his most ambitious project. In this unfinished work he stated his intention of freeing himself completely from the biographical element.[11] This remark should probably be interpreted to mean the exclusion of obviously autobiographical matter; if one may judge by the completed first part, Doderer's own experiences, however transmuted, would still have provided a basic element. Fortunately, this first volume, *Die Wasserfälle von Slunj* (1963), is one of his most successful works; it can be read, as now indeed it must be read, as an autonomous unit. Further, it supports Doderer's own contention that plot is still (or again) important, that the novel must reconquer the realm of outer reality.[12]

Even more than the comedy of manners, the novel tends to be associated with great cities—London, Paris, St. Petersburg, Vienna, New York, Berlin—or with smaller but substantial centers like Dublin, Lübeck, or Boston. If this is true, it is most unlikely that the novel will wither away in an "urban-secular" age like ours. No other contemporary form has the scope to deal with so large a scene.

With its mixture of comic and tragic elements, *Die Wasserfälle von Slunj* seems to hold a unique place in the author's work. Often Doderer tended to follow the tradition of the educational novel, by definition an optimistic subgenre; *Die Strudlhofstiege* is Doderer's most successful *Bildungsroman.* At the other end of the spectrum is located his grandiose account of the "Cannae of Austrian freedom," *The Demons. Die Wasserfälle von Slunj* contains most of Doderer's typical themes, but its central character, Donald Clayton, leads a life of frustration and failure. Only such relatively minor characters as Chwostik and Münsterer become genuine human beings, undergoing the process of becoming human (*Menschwerdung*) which plays a central part in Doderer's work from *Every Man a Murderer* on. Caught like Kafka's protagonists in self-centered, rootless bachelorhood, Clayton fails the woman who loves him and lapses into a black depression. His belated efforts to reverse the situation only hasten his end. (While the occasion of his death is accidental, it is completely clear that he has lost the will to live.) Clayton's image of himself as the gentlemanly, disengaged bachelor is his particular form of that "second reality" against which Doderer repeatedly warned his readers. As Ernst Erich Noth has pointed out, the "second reality" is the sphere of fanatic ideology or some other obsession; it is actually unreal.[13] Piero Rismondo makes virtually the same point in different words: reality is made by God, the "second reality" by man.[14]

Not surprisingly, Vienna, the mountains of Austria and Serbia (as it was then called), and the Hungarian plains are sensuously and skillfully presented. Doderer gives us, as he does in *Die Strudlhofstiege*, the very aura of the Austrian capital; he presents a large cast of Viennese persons, mainly admirable or at least tolerable like the amiable prostitutes Finy and Faverl, plus the one Viennese type he loathed, the concierge and his even more deadly female analogue, *die Hausmeisterin.* Yet it would be most misleading to see in Doderer only or primarily another champion of "Old Vienna," *Austria felix* (*infelix?*), Franz Joseph, and all that. If at times sentimental, Doderer was neither uncritical nor provincial about his native country. Basically cosmopolitan, he was captivated by the lure of Siberian forests and Russian plains; and he shared the Anglophilia of so many Continental Europeans. Although he wrote of England as "that island we all revere and love," he was not unaware of the human coldness of a certain sort of Anglo-Saxon; indeed, the protagonist of *Die Wasserfälle von Slunj* illustrates this defect. Above all, Doderer was a highly educated person, expert in Austrian history and so versed in the classics that, not content with numerous allusions, he coined Latin phrases of his own, like *conciergificatio.*[15] His brief, highly stimulating *Grundlagen und Funktion des Romans* ("Foundations and Function of the Novel"—1959) demonstrates familiarity with international practice and theory—with Goethe, Joyce, Proust, Thomas Mann, E. M. Forster, and Lawrence, and with Lukács and Wolfgang Kayser.

Die Wasserfälle von Slunj shows the meticulous planning and plotting we have come to expect of Doderer. Like an architect or an engineer, he charted out the skeleton of his actions on a drawing board before he wrote his books. Characters are linked, sometimes by coincidence, with a number of others. Of course it is no accident that Donald Clayton finds his death in the great waterfalls of Slunj, near the place he was begotten. Some readers feel that Doderer's books are too consciously constructed, his characters too obviously manipulated[16]—a point to which we must return.

In style as well as theme, "The Waterfalls of Slunj" often recalls earlier works of Doderer but has an individuality of its own. Although he is not a realist in the conventional sense, he imparts an extraordinary semblance of reality. While his novels may be described as rich orchestrations of precisely conceived, almost geometric structures, the luxuriance of his style recalls Marianne Moore's metaphorical definition of poetry: imaginary gardens inhabited by real toads.

As in *Die Strudlhofstiege* and elsewhere, Doderer offers a wealth of sense perceptions. ("Apperception" is a key term in his theory of fiction.) Odors are important to him: in describing an early morning in the Prater he notes the smell of the tanbark, of stagnant water, and of vegetation. He is equally sensitive to light and color, noting the "reflection of the green treetops" in a room or describing the impact of bright sunshine on a man who has just begun to look forward with confidence to the future: "The sun [was] like a plane of gold effortlessly penetrating him; the blue window was a second entering light; the white ship was the third." [17]

Although Doderer's style is less baroque in *Die Wasserfälle von Slunj* than elsewhere,[18] he revels in rhetorical devices. Occasionally he uses alliterations like "under the thick slime stratum of his shame" (p. 56). Absolute constructions and rhetorical questions remind one of his debt to Latin prose. He makes a rather sparing use of leitmotifs like "the Prater's steaming meadow" (pp. 141 ff.). Besides reproducing Viennese dialect and employing even Czech and Hungarian terms, usually with humorous effect, he has a strong tendency to use words which clearly derive from French or Latin. As in Hofmannsthal's *Der Schwierige* ("The Difficult Man"), the implication is that such so-called "foreign words" are genuinely and typically Austrian.

Metaphors and similes are interwoven skillfully into the fabric of the language. Such "baroque" oxymora as "a hot glacier" (p. 226—used of a passionate woman) are rare, but other striking images abound, especially at moments of tension. When Clayton realizes his love for Monica Bachler, she is "already imbedded in him, like an arrow"; when she makes an encouraging remark, it affects him "like letting down a bridge, a boarding bridge"; later her absence "yawned beside him, . . . a cold, empty gap" (pp. 193, 194, 195). A disappointed lover identifies himself with the cast-off heel of a shoe, half-covered by the dust of the highway. A few images have symbolic quality, above all the waterfalls themselves, evoked near the beginning and at the end of the novel. Around them the earth trembles; linked with love, procreation, and death, they suggest an ultimate reality. Donald's collapse at the falls recalls the failure of a very different type of lover, Mynheer Peeperkorn, when his voice is drowned out by the waterfall near the Magic Mountain.

Doderer makes very free use—at times too free [19]—of the author's privilege to intervene. At least twice he explicitly banishes characters from the book—first Finy and Faverl, then the dreadful *Hausmeisterin* Frau Wewerka—though the two girls are later readmitted. He likes to include punctuation marks in parentheses thus, (?!)—to indicate the narrator's attitude, briefly implying affection or the reverse, and to make such half-serious comments as "The reader and the author get dreadfully worried"

(p. 348). With very self-conscious romantic irony he lists a certain Doderer as a member of one of the classes at a Viennese *Gymnasium* (p. 229). Such interventions are not to everyone's taste but seem appropriate in novels with a large comic or ironic element. The works of Fielding and Wieland are distinguished precedents.

On almost every page Doderer's characteristic wit and humor flash out. He scorns neither the pun nor the belly laugh but is most characteristic in sophisticated aphorisms. In their later years, he notes, men do not scorn the erotic pearls cast before them (p. 253). Women who advise others in affairs of the heart are "mainly dead-drunk on common sense" (p. 311). Actual drinkers, however, "are always more humane than nondrinkers. They are easier to talk to, and when they can't talk any more, that's better still" (p. 339). In the art of naming, Doderer is almost as inventive as Thomas Mann: persons called Wenidoppler, Okrogelnik, Finy and Faverl, Frau Wewerka, and Frau Krulow, née Wustenstiebel—she rides through the desert dust on a donkey—are to some extent characterized before they do or say anything.

Predominantly interested in the structure of his novels, Doderer generally presents his characters in low relief rather than in the round.[20] This is not necessarily a defect; and in any case, at least two figures—Monica and Donald—are three-dimensional. The novelist has made the transfer of Monica Bachler's affections from Donald Clayton to his father (an extremely brief affair with Chwostik intervenes) admirably credible. And as already indicated, the account of Donald's crucial blunder (chargeable to a lack of imagination, to sexual cowardice, or both) and of his ensuing decline and fall is very convincing. When he desperately tries to blot out the memory of his past defeat by forcing his attentions on another woman, we know that he is lost.

Perhaps the one serious defect of the book is that its actors and actions are too predictable. One senses all too soon that Chwostik will succeed, that Donald is doomed. Writing of Turgenev, Henry James rightly held that a novelist's figures must maintain their autonomy as individuals:

No one has more of that sign of the born novelist which resides in a respect unconditioned for the freedom and vitality, the absoluteness when summoned, of the creatures he invokes; or is more superior to the strange and second-rate policy of explaining or presenting them by reprobation or apology,—of taking the short cuts and anticipating the emotions and judgments about them that should be left, at the best, to the perhaps not most intelligent reader.[21]

James's view is an extreme one, but Doderer does tend to explain too much: his characters rarely surprise us. Usually they follow the course which his keen intelligence has charted for them in advance. Despite all their charm, they move, not like marionettes, but like dancers in an elaborate ballet.

This limitation, of course, by no means invalidates "The Waterfalls of Slunj" as an aesthetic structure. Fortunately, the distinction between books that are "made" and those that "grow organically" is no longer fashionable. The division must rather be made between works which are true to their own intention and inherent principles, as "The Waterfalls of Slunj" is, and the many which are not. Even as conservative a critic as Emil Staiger holds that a work has style when all its components, formal and thematic, are consonant. The bourgeois tragicomedy of Donald Clayton, presented in a largely comic but not unserious setting, possesses its own characteristic consonance. Doderer's technique of narration, only "apparently conventional,"[22] may seem, after Mann, Broch, and Musil, too much concerned with the mere surfaces of reality, but the author himself has anticipated this possible objection: "For this world is completely contained in its lovely surface, including all its 'depths' (especially its depths), and let whoever does not believe this please ask a painter." [23]

7 / Squaring the Circle: Hermann Broch's *The Sleepwalkers*

> "Modern literature is never sheer poetry but always science and philosophy too."
>
> —Walter Jens

Walter Jens's statement that modern literature always contains elements of science and philosophy is reminiscent of Friedrich Schlegel's proclamation of a universal, all-embracing poetry. It illuminates one aspect of modern literature very well, but it is clearly debatable. It does apply though to a great many twentieth-century writers—to none more than to Hermann Broch. Broch's whole career as a novelist and sociologist was dominated by a heroic determination to reach the truth, *Erkenntnis*, knowledge in its totality. If he never quite squared the circle, he did at his best achieve approximations of total experience in its rational and nonrational elements. The most representative of his grandiose approximations are, I believe, his trilogy, *The Sleepwalkers* (1931–1932), and *The Death of Virgil* (1945).

Broch's modernity is not a matter of chronology. Whether or not his novels are "beyond Joyce and Kafka," as Heinz Politzer has argued,[1] they display many or most of the characteristics one associates with the modern narrative: devaluation of plot and of the hero, and rejection of the ordinary concepts of time. Like Joyce and Mann, Broch was engaged in the search for a new form making use of musical devices or of myth, or both.[2] His works evince a close knowledge of Freudian psychology but also attempt to transcend all psychologizing. (It is relevant that the contemporary novelists he most valued were Joyce and Kafka.) Like Kafka, he was fascinated by the irruption of nonrational forces into a seemingly secure world; like Gide, he was concerned with gratuitous acts.

Thus the three volumes of *The Sleepwalkers* (*1888: Pasenow or Romanticism; 1903: Esch or Anarchy;* and *1918: Huguenau or Objectivity*) are not primarily intended as historical depiction. To be sure, as the precise dates in their titles emphasize, they are concerned with a historical development and tell us a great deal about the course of German society, but their intention is much broader.

Before turning to Broch's theory of the novel, one needs at least a tentative answer to the question: Who are these "somnambulists"? Not only the romantic puritan Joachim von Pasenow and the confused sectarian August Esch, but also the brutally realistic Wilhelm Huguenau and the highly intelligent Eduard von Bertrand are caught up in dreams. (Sheer rationality can be even more dangerous than sheer irrationality, Broch held.) So, aside from a few brief moments, are all the figures in this broad panorama. Huguenau is blind to moral values; Bertrand, an aesthete in the pejorative sense, has no genuine concern with human beings. Yet a somnambulist, precisely because he is unaware of immediate events, may reach genuine insight.[3] This is rare: in the trilogy a whole society—Junkers, capitalists, petty bourgeois, "outsiders," the officers and men of the army, and so on—is walking in its sleep. As the years pass, the tone darkens: the illusions of romanticism are replaced by the frenzy of anarchy; anarchy gives way to nihilistic objectivity (*Sachlichkeit*). Values and reality are corroded.

"Does this distorted life still possess reality? Does this hypertrophied reality still possess life?" Broch asks.[4] Yet, having great faith in dialectics, he managed to extract a measure of comfort from the fact that the contemporary world could get no worse; an antithetical reaction was overdue.

As the last point suggests, Broch was a systematic thinker, devoted to theory and to the philosophy of history. Often this devotion seems excessive; but it is partially offset by a skeptical, empirical element of his mind. Like the hero of Musil's *Man without Qualities*, he rated both "precision" and "soul" highly. *The Sleepwalkers* flows from his general view of the world, in which art and literature, particularly the novel, played an important part. In fact the essayistic sections of *Huguenau* provide an explicit commentary on the whole trilogy.

Loathing *l'art pour l'art* and literature as entertainment, Broch believed strongly that the novel must be an instrument for determining the truth, comparable in value to science and philosophy; otherwise it has no right to exist. It must provide, not historical pictures of an era, but philosophically valid "models."[5] Like Friedrich Hebbel, an equally implacable Hegelian, he was interested in history less for its own sake than for its revelation of how the dialectics of change work in a critical period. Unlike Hebbel, however, he had an ardent concern with his own age; and he included himself, by clear implication, among the sleepwalkers. That age he saw as one of deep decline and radical hope, in which messianic expectations coexist with utter amorality.

To approximate the totality of the epoch in fiction, Broch mobilized a multiplicity of forms and styles, as Joyce had done in *Ulysses*.[6] *The Sleepwalkers* moves on three levels: that of external action and those of the psychological and of what Broch called the "epistemological," including matters of which the characters are not themselves aware; it is a sort of commentary given by an "ideal narrator" (*Erzähler als Idee*[7]—Broch's terms are often formidable). *The Sleepwalkers* has three narrators; the stance of each is indicated in the trilogy by the subtitle of the given section: thus the particular narrator comprehends and yet transcends romanticism, anarchy, and nihilistic realism in turn. Every person, every incident in a "model" must be related to the supernarrator.

Theoretically, the "epistemological" novel presents not only the actions and thoughts of its characters, but objective, impersonal truth in the comments of the ideal narrator. These at least are the deductions which Kreutzer makes in his very able commentary on *The Sleepwalkers*.[8] Yet at times, at least, Broch realized that he could at best approach absolute truth in his "polyhistoric" and "polyphonic" novels, as he called them. Since times of decay—the term is used neutrally here—do not understand themselves, any more than the contemporaries of Goethe and Beethoven understood *Faust II* or the "last quartets," a relatively ideal narrator, who may approximate the truth, is necessary.[9] Similarly, an "agglomeration" of styles produces "the highest measure of reality"[10]—not necessarily complete reality. Broch's commentator, if suspiciously like the old-fashioned "omniscient narrator" in some respects, normally confines himself to philosophical and sociological generalizations.

Neither the commentary nor the action leaves any doubt that society has entered a catastrophic phase. At the end of the trilogy Huguenau, having murdered Esch, takes up his career as a businessman again; his utter amorality seems to guarantee his success. Pasenow becomes insane. No values survive except survival itself, and reality has lost meaning. All coherence is indeed gone. Yet by a dialectical leap of faith Broch reached the conclusion that an age in which all standards had disappeared would—inevitably?—bring forth values of its own. Thus there is even hope in and for Huguenau,[11] the most unpleasant figure in the trilogy. Here Broch seems indebted to Nietzsche's notion that decadence is the precondition of the emergence of a new man. At the end, however, Broch turns to the Bible rather than to philosophy: "Do thyself no harm, for we are all here!"[12]

1888: Pasenow or Romanticism

To the casual reader, *Pasenow* may seem an attractive but rather unremarkable novel which follows the tradition of Fontane, Eduard von Keyserling, and Mann's *Buddenbrooks* without making any particular contribution of its own. As in Fontane, we encounter the Prussian milieu and the theme of mésalliance; as in Keyserling, the gentle melancholy of aristocratic decadence; as in Mann, the decline of a family. Broch successfully recreates action and mood; he observes the Iron Cross earned by an earlier Pasenow in the Wars of Liberation displayed "framed, under glass," on the wall of the family manor. His account of Joachim von Pasenow's wedding day has the muted tone typical of many neoromantic novelists of the end of the century:

> It was a quiet wedding. His father's condition was unchanged; he lived in a daze, no longer perceived the world around him, and one had to face the fact that things could go on like this

for years. To be sure, his mother said that a quiet, intimate celebration was more to her taste and her husband's than brilliant parties.[13]

This is very well done but, for a novel written around 1930, very conventional. The action indeed is deliberately traditional, even trite: a well-meaning, rather weak young man of good family loves a lower-class girl of dubious background; his passion is requited and fulfilled. Influenced partly by a rather cynical friend and more by his own inhibitions, he abandons the warm-hearted girl to marry a "pure" young woman of his own caste. This is hardly a fresh theme; Fontane had treated such situations at least equally well, some fifty years before.

Yet *Pasenow* is by no means an anachronism; it has values of its own. The second part of the subtitle gives an important hint; the protagonist is a romantic, in the sense indicated in the novel itself: "And as it is always romanticism when earthly things are raised to absolutes, the severe, particular romanticism of this age is the cult of the uniform" (p. 19). Later in the book, Broch gives a more concise definition: "a person who is afraid of knowledge—that is, a romanticist" (p. 475). The Prussian system, then, is itself romantic. Thus Pasenow's friend Eduard von Bertrand compares the atmosphere of the army to that of a circus and cannot understand how "two men can . . . shoot at each other . . . in a world of machines and railways" (p. 53). Joachim's brother has just been killed in a duel.

Joachim von Pasenow's romanticism, closely linked to a sort of Prussian puritanism, determines much of the action. Thus he is afraid of sex; his relations with his Czech mistress Ruzena make him feel especially sinful. Reacting against this passion, he comes to see Elisabeth, whom he later marries, as a sexless madonna. Actually, she is by no means a disembodied spirit, but he is compelled "to raise earthly things to an absolute" and to interpret her inexperience as saintliness. Similarly, he is afraid of new ideas, and hence sees his intelligent acquaintance Bertrand as a Mephistopheles. (That Bertrand has resigned his commission in the army disturbs Joachim even more than the fact that Ruzena is a Czech.) Appropriately, he fears civilian life: his uniform is "a second skin," a suit of armor, indeed a cage. Actually, Joachim, a basically attractive person, never wanted to enter the army or otherwise to follow the example of his father, whom he loathes—with good reason. In his case, at least, romanticism is the opium of the weak.

Broch has avoided the conventional antithesis between the loving lower-class girl and the cold, aristocratic lady by making Elisabeth a complex and interesting person. She is magnetically drawn to Bertrand, who has divined her latent sensuality. Poor Pasenow is too naïve to do this, and his wedding trip with her is ludicrously—and pathetically—chaste. Broch, however, ends the novel with a four-sentence "chapter" which alienates us from "romanticism" completely, if unsubtly:

Nevertheless, they had their first child after about eighteen months. It just happened. It is not necessary to tell how this came about. After the materials supplied about the structure of the characters, the reader can work it out himself [p. 170].

Joachim's father, arrogant, embittered, and half-crazy, is one of those portraits of Prussian types which often appear in Austrian literature. Compared to him, Musil's Arnheim and Hofmannsthal's Neuhoff are pleasant gentlemen. The special bitterness of Broch's characterization seems to derive from an unhappy relation to his own father.[14]

Eduard von Bertrand is a more attractive figure; he is intelligent, pleasant, and well-behaved. Yet as Ruzena's instinctive rejection of Bertrand suggests, Joachim is not entirely wrong to distrust him. He behaves correctly but seems to regard other persons as objects, at best as patients on whom operations must be performed. "He talk[s] like a physician" (p. 119), Joachim feels, when Bertrand is discussing Ruzena's future. As has been noted, Bertrand sees through the romanticism of the Prussian establishment, but he is an aesthete like Hofmannsthal's Claudio, in *Death and the Fool,* related subtly to the sphere of Wilde, Beardsley, D'Annunzio, and Stefan George. As this attitude was anathema to Broch, it is fitting that Bertrand plays an important, if basically negative role in the second part of *The Sleepwalkers,* and indirectly in the third. He has been called the "passive hero" of the whole work.[15]

The style of *Pasenow* gives another important indication of the book's intention. As noted, the style itself often appears romantic: "In the evenings he keeps thinking of Ruzena. There are evenings whose twilight lasts much longer than is astronomically prescribed. Then a smoky, thin mist sinks over the city" (p. 24). Yet this style derives largely from the fact that the reader is led to see things through Pasenow's eyes or through the eyes of the "ideal narrator," or more often through a combination of both. Thus the words "than is astronomically prescribed" supply a cool, antiromantic note. When Pasenow, in love with Ruzena, feels "carried away, as if the longing which filled him were a soft, gentle flowing of his heart" (p. 38), the "as if" distances the reader. Pasenow likes experiences which produce "an agreeable sadness" in him (p. 116). Broch's leitmotifs at times not only characterize but criticize. The phrase "indolence of feeling" (*Trägheit des Gefühls*) casts light on both Bertrand and Pasenow. Perhaps it may derive from Jacob Wassermann's "indolence of the heart," a central theme in his *Caspar Hauser*. While the point of view is generally modified by virtue of its being more or less that of Pasenow, the ideal narrator occasionally speaks entirely in his own right. Pasenow's devotion to the uniform is analyzed in a complicated twelve-line sentence which he could never have composed (p. 23). Similarly, the reason that Elisabeth's parents are compulsive collectors—every collector tries to reach infinity, we are told, by achieving absolute completeness and thus "overcoming his death" (p. 74)—goes far beyond her or their comprehension.

Because of Broch's unusually sensitive empathy, even for characters of whom he disapproves, his irony is veiled and seldom has a chilling effect. We sympathize with Joachim, with Ruzena's spontaneous reactions, with Bertrand in his isolation. Only old Pasenow—a caricature à la George Grosz—is beyond the pale. Well-acquainted with Freud's theories, Broch makes the limitations of Joachim's love apparent by simply mentioning the times he forgets to give Ruzena the laces he has bought for her. Old Pasenow commits the ghastliest of Freudian slips in failing to recognize his own son, returned to the family estate for his brother's funeral. Hostility can go no further.

Although Broch's overriding moral concern is less obvious in *Pasenow* than in his later works, it is still clear. "Indolence of feeling" may very well be a concomitant of romantic *Schwärmerei;* the latter appears as a compensation for a basic human failure. When the ideal narrator notes that the sense of security a uniform gives isolates the soldier from the ordinary concerns of men, he adds, "for the secure life is based on intolerance and misunderstanding" (p. 20). *Pasenow* is not after all a nostalgic evocation of the old Prussian system; it is a severe though by no means bitter judgment on it.

1903: Esch or Anarchy

Anarchy dominates the characters, the action, and to some extent the style of the second volume; this motif is more richly orchestrated than is the theme of romanticism in *Pasenow*. To Esch, the unintellectual protagonist, "anarchy" means that "no one knows whether he stands to the right or the left, on this side or that" (p. 248). For reasons he cannot fathom, people seem forced to spend their lives in occupations they find repellent: the severely correct Mother Hentjen runs a tavern; the pietistic Lohberg sells tobacco. Esch himself is associated with a troupe of female wrestlers. Although he realizes that their performances appeal to the crudest sexuality, he persists in this venture for respectable, even idealistic motives. Significantly, he never achieves his goal. For the ideal narrator, anarchy pertains to the decay of values and of men. The intellectual scene at the end of the century was indeed chaotic; as Musil put it, "If one had dissected that epoch, some such nonsense would have resulted as an angular circle consisting of wooden iron." [16] To Broch, anarchy was a necessary precondition of true ethical freedom: neither moralistic dogmatism nor aestheticism was viable. "Can a new ethic arise from the sleep and the dreams of the nastiest everyday reality?" [17] He leaves the question open.

The action of *Esch* is deliberately inconclusive; though a gifted teller of tales, Broch had no respect whatever for the conventional novel.[18] The protagonist Esch involves himself in a series of generally sordid events in order to realize his quixotic ends. Endowed with a strong sense of justice, he tries in vain to take vengeance on two men he considers evil. Similarly, his attempt to save Ilona, an entertainer of less than dubious character, from having to take part in a knife-throwing spectacle, is frustrated, as is his wish to emigrate to America, which symbolizes the freedom he confusedly seeks throughout. Basically, he is a likable person; one feels that Broch on the whole approved of him.[19]

Esch is a complicated but credible figure, earthy but basically religious, both a bookkeeper and a visionary. As a bookkeeper, he feels that the world does not "add up"; it is his intuition of injustice and absurdity which makes him seek for salvation. Still a romantic, he finds only a "half-solution . . . in erotic mysticism."[20] He is obsessed with thoughts of sacrifice and has a sort of crucifixion complex: he associates Ilona, as the knives strike the screen to which she is bound, with Jesus, though in a less exalted mood, he realizes that she is a low creature. Throughout, he is doubly motivated; his fascination with Mother Hentjen, whom he eventually marries, combines sheer physicality with hopes of redemption. Like Alfred Döblin's Franz Biberkopf, he is a rather dim-witted seeker for the truth. He is "on the right road but not the right man for the road," to quote Thomas Mann out of context.[21]

Bertrand, who appears again in the second volume, is far less vividly realized than is Esch. In fact, he is deliberately kept indistinct,[22] for Broch, focusing more and more on symbolic values, increasingly slights verisimilitude as the novel proceeds. He tends to "go beyond" psychology as well as action—a somewhat risky procedure for a novelist. Like Pasenow, Esch feels a moral aversion for Bertrand; in the latter case this is far more irrational, for Esch has never suffered any injury from Bertrand, who is now a fabulously successful businessman. Although Esch may be right in linking him with the injustices of capitalism, he sees in him a fundamental religious threat. Obsessed with theological archetypes, the protagonist associates Bertrand with the anti-Christ or Gnostic "anti-God" who must be destroyed.[23] During his encounter with Bertrand—which is very probably hallucinatory [24]—Esch's hatred gives way to love. Near the end of the novel, he reads of Bertrand's suicide in a newspaper.

In the account of Esch's passion for Mother Hentjen, Broch's disengagement from "mere" psychology is most evident. She was older than he, avoided men, and was without apparent charms of body or mind, but he pursued her doggedly and finally overcame her resistance. When she at last yielded,

> he felt such bliss as he had never experienced with a woman before, . . . longing to possess her, who was no longer "she" but motherly life given again, wrested from the unknown, extinguishing the "I" which has broken through its boundaries, vanished and submerged in its own freedom. For the man who wills the good and the just wills the absolute, and Esch perceived for the first time that it is not a matter of pleasure but of union [p. 274].

Similarly, the homosexual Harry tells him:

> Love is a great strangeness [*Fremdheit*]: there are two people and each is on a different star and neither can ever know anything of the other. And suddenly there is no distance any longer and no time and they have plunged so deep into each other that they know nothing more of themselves or each other and do not need to know any more. That is love [p. 283].

In Esch's case this passion is, however irrationally founded, not evanescent or anonymous; he feels, like Mother Hentjen, that it will endure throughout their lives. Broch seems to imply far more than the drastic resolution of an Oedipus complex; this is more myth than psychology. Mother Hentjen, he wrote "is 'value-free' [*wertfrei*] and autonomous, just as the 'feminine' or 'nature' is as such always value-free."[25]

In the passage describing Esch's ecstasy, we hear again the voice of the ideal narrator, putting into words what a given figure could not himself formulate. To balance such flights, Broch also includes the brutal side of the relation. Esch often beats his wife, not without some provocation, but the last sentence of this part of the trilogy reads, "He still beat her often, but less and less and finally stopped completely" (p. 366). Esch's "erotic mysticism" turns out to be, even for him personally, a partial and thus unsatisfactory solution. In the third novel, Esch becomes a sort of lay preacher; eroticism sinks into the background.

Two levels of style, one realistic, the other "explosive," as Broch put it,[26] correspond to the two sides of Esch's nature and to the apparent orderliness and essential anarchy of the epoch. Tavern and workshop scenes contrast with the surrealistic tone of Esch's metaphysical conversation with Bertrand. It is almost certainly a dream: Bertrand has been expecting this visitor, calls him "child," and discusses the very matters which have obsessed Esch, above all the belief that the world must undergo apocalyptic convulsions before a new era begins (p. 234).

Clearly, Esch's moral fanaticism is shown more sympathetically than is Pasenow's retreat into romanticism. Fanaticism represents a long step forward—toward the abyss, but also toward that potential salvation which Esch expects and in which the ideal commentator, like Broch himself, has placed his last hope. One need not be an "aesthete" to feel that the commentary becomes too explicit, that the subtler approach of *Pasenow* is more effective; but of course this increased emphasis on direct moral statement was an integral part of Broch's design. In any case, this objection can best be discussed at the end of this chapter.

1918: Huguenau or Objectivity

In *Huguenau*, the apocalypse seems to be at hand. The war has not actually caused the decay of values and the collapse of German society, but it has vastly accelerated the plunge downward. The dissolution of the individual is most frightening of all: it is as if the pressures of the age had fractured men's psyches—a psychological splitting of the atom. The anti-Christ is at hand, perhaps in the person of Huguenau.

As if to emphasize the centrifugal quality of the time, Broch includes five distinct actions: the career of Huguenau, in which Esch and Joachim von Pasenow (who appears as an aging, devoutly religious officer) are deeply involved; the story of a Salvation Army girl in Berlin (completely separate in plot, though not in theme, from the rest of the novel); the events centering in an army hospital; the account of Hannah Wendling's psychological withdrawal from the persons around her; and the bizarre history of Gödicke, long robbed of all consciousness by war injuries, who gradually revives and feels himself literally reborn.

In these actions, decay and hope are counterpointed. On the one hand, Huguenau's success is the triumph of sheer dehumanization; the army hospital mirrors the destruction of man, moral as well as physical; and Hannah Wendling's isolation is symptomatic of a spreading neurosis. As values disintegrate, reality and the sense of identity wither. On the other hand, the groping religiosity of the Salvation Army, of the grotesque Gödicke, and of Esch show that at least the search for values is continuing.

These narratives, then, serve as examples, as specimens, as the parables in Broch's sermon. Its core is the long essay "Decay of Values," divided into ten sections which are interspersed at irregular but frequent intervals. There is much further commentary in the Salvation Army episodes, attributed to a fictive narrator, Dr. Bertrand Müller.[27] (In a chaotic epoch, the ideal narrator may speak through more than one mask.) Thus a considerable percentage of the eighty-eight sections of *Huguenau* and parts of others are devoted to nonnarrative ends. Implacably didactic, Broch includes his views on the Renaissance and his cardinal epistemological theories. These passages are not integrated into the action as are, say, the excursuses on time in *The Magic Mountain* or Stephen Dedalus' ideas in *Portrait of the Artist as a Young Man.* If *Ulysses*, in Harry Levin's much-quoted words, is "a novel to end all novels,"[28] one may well ask if *Huguenau* is a novel at all. Of course the question of genre is very different from the question of rank.

Besides employing narrative, connected essays, and brief aphorisms, Broch casts one section dramatically ("The Symposium, or Conversation, on Salvation") and frequently uses verse in the Salvation Army section. Although one would hardly call the "Symposium" genuinely dramatic or the verses particularly lyrical, they do contribute to the centrifugal intention of the work. Similarly, Broch includes various hymns—one with the significantly recurring line "Send the fire!"—and quotes in full some of Huguenau's nefarious business letters and contracts.

In parts of the novel, the tone is as objective as the subtitle leads one to expect; elsewhere, as in the "Symposium," it has expressionistic fervor. As Broch put it, this novel is "in a sense reportage," but narrative form as such is "ruptured," in line with "the complete collapse of the old values." [29]

The last phrase brings one back to Huguenau, the representative man of the epoch. On a moral level, his "objectivity" is sheer nihilism. With no twinges of conscience, he deserts from the army, makes his way by swindling and intrigue, does much to drive Pasenow to a breakdown, and kills Esch almost immediately after sleeping with the latter's wife.[30] After the war he returns home, where he becomes a respected personage, although his fellow citizens tend to avoid him. On a human, or better, a dehumanized level he is indeed the anti-Christ foreseen by Esch. Yet precisely because he is autonomous and "value-free," Broch finds hope in his emergence. Since Huguenau knows no moral bonds, his life has the "form of freedom, within which alone the new content can arise." [31] It was thus consistent that Broch could suggest that a moral rebirth might well emerge from the Nazi era.[32] Huguenau, like evil itself, may be regarded as playing the role of Goethe's Mephistopheles:

> A part of that power
> Which always wills evil, and always makes for good.

Reflecting that the decades after Hitler's fall have hardly been notable for moral renascence, one is led to the melancholy conclusion that dialectical logic is not infallible.

Looking back over the trilogy, one perceives that numerous linking factors hold it together, if not always tautly. Important figures reappear: Pasenow, Esch and his wife, and Bertrand. The leitmotifs, especially those of sacrifice and salvation, have a similar function. Above all, of course, the concern with values and reality gives the work its moral unity. From that point of view, the three "times" of the action flow into one (the dates 1888–1918 are precisely those of Wilhelm II's reign); the span of thirty years appears as a single, catastrophic development.

Unquestionably the intention of *The Sleepwalkers* is clear, its aim noble and important. Is it a completely successful work of art? One's doubts do not flow from the fear that it bears too heavy a weight of meaning—after all, Broch's own *The Death of Virgil* does sustain such a burden with at least relative success. Rather, the different aspects and levels of the book do not seem to be sufficiently interrelated. Goethe's statement in his *Maxims and Reflections* is relevant here: "Symbols transform the phenomenon into the idea, the idea into an image; and in such a way that the idea within the image always remains infinitely effective and inachievable." [33] Too often, in *The Sleepwalkers*, the idea is not immanent in the image; if it were, there would be less need for essayistic commentary.[34]

If we regard the trilogy from the viewpoint of philosophy or of prophecy, other doubts arise. It is, at least in part, too "dialectic": it is hard to believe that Huguenau is somehow preparing the way, however inadvertently, for better things. We *know* that he and the age are evil; the rest is speculation. Perhaps Robert Musil had something like this in mind when he wrote, "Broch makes one suspicious of the philosophical novel." [35] Beautiful as the words of biblical consolation quoted in the trilogy's last sentence are—"Do thyself no harm, for we are all here!"—they apply only in a limited sense: while man himself, in a reduced sense, survives, the old values do not, and new ones have not appeared, as Broch has demonstrated in overwhelming and convincing detail.

Of course Broch's purpose was to show all the elements of a period, rational and irrational, through a whole range of styles, to convey the blackness of the age and yet the hope of a fundamental redemption. He was quite aware that he could not completely realize his intention. "Squaring the circle? Certainly, that is what the poet's job is," he wrote to Frank Thiess.[36] At least one novelist came closer than Broch to approximating the solution of an equally difficult problem: Thomas Mann's *Doctor Faustus* presents an even darker epoch; it too ends on the note of hope. Mann's consolation, however, is a muted one, more subtly expressed and hence more credible: describing the ending of Leverkühn's last composition, the narrator speaks of "hope beyond hopelessness"; the last note, "which was the final expression of sadness, is that no more; [it] changes its sense, stands as a light in the night."[37] Furthermore, by using the technique of the "magic square,"[38] Mann managed really to integrate the various actions and levels of his novel.

In his famous essay on Joyce, Broch states that the true artist puts the good before the beautiful; the opposite procedure results in *Kitsch*.[39] (The term is revealingly harsh: whatever reservations one may have about the early poetry of Stefan George or the writings of Oscar Wilde, they are hardly trash.) Here Broch ran the great risk of underrating the function of art in his revulsion from aestheticism—"Incidit in Scyllam, qui vult vitare Charybdim" (The man who wishes to avoid Charybdis falls victim to Scylla). It is curious that an avowed Platonist like Broch failed to realize that beauty and truth may be aspects of the same entity. At any rate, although Broch took great pains with the shape of the trilogy—the contrapuntal arrangement of the eighty-eight sections of *Huguenau* is particularly striking evidence

—his low estimate of the formal element seems to have left some traces in the novel. Presumably, lyrical insertions should be genuinely lyrical, as they are in Goethe's novels. They need not of course be in verse: one thinks of *Ulysses* or of *Tonio Kröger*.

Though a highly gifted novelist, Broch clearly assigned too low a value to form. To be sure, his afterword to *Die Schuldlosen* "The Innocents") contains a fine vindication of the novel as a genre. Unlike science, it can present totalities, "man in his wholeness." Although it cannot convert men or give them specific moral lessons, it does contribute to a "process of purification." [40] This vindication is admirable as far as it goes, but it focuses entirely on the purpose of literature and neglects ways and means. To return to Jens's statement that modern literature includes philosophy and science, one would add the precondition that these elements must themselves be transmuted into literature.

Whatever the flaws of this very rich book, *The Sleepwalkers* remains impressive as a picture and a diagnosis of a time. For a writer like Broch, who set himself so lofty a goal, one feels admiration and intellectual affection. Since he cited Goethe's drive for universality as a basic part of the modern writer's inheritance,[41] it seems appropriate to end with a line from *Faust*—one loves the man who strives to achieve the impossible—Goethe suggests:

> Den lieb' ich, der Unmögliches begehrt.

8/ The Artist as Satirist: Günter Grass

Getauft geimpft gefirmt geschult.
Gespielt hab ich mit Bombensplittern.
Und aufgewachsen bin ich zwischen
dem Heilgen Geist und Hitlers Bild.

(Baptized, vaccinated, confirmed, schooled
I played with bomb splinters
And I grew up between
the Holy Ghost and Hitler's picture.)
—Günter Grass, "Kleckerburg" [1]

Of the many new writers who emerged in Germany after the nightmare ended in 1945, Günter Grass is one of the most talented—a writer with a spectacular flair for language, image, and metaphor. Grass's international renown is based primarily on his prose fiction, but he has written lyrics and a number of plays and dramatic sketches as well, to say nothing of his achievements in the graphic arts and sculpture. In this chapter, I shall confine myself to his two long novels, *The Tin Drum* (1959) and *Dog Years* (1963), with a few words about his intervening story *Cat and Mouse* (1961).

In all these works, Danzig and the surrounding region, including the rivers and the Baltic, play an important part. As a native of the former Free City, he regards Germany from a certain distance; his books are written from the point of view of a semioutsider, though as a citizen he plays an active political role. His attitude toward Poland and the

Polish element in Danzig is warm and sympathetic. As Grass puts it in his brief poem "Nächtliches Stadion" ("Nocturnal Stadium"):

> Einsam stand der Dichter im Tor,
> doch der Schiedsrichter pfiff: Abseits—[2]
>
> (The poet stood, solitary, at the goal
> but the referee whistled, "Offside"—)

Born in 1927, shortly before Hitler became a formidable threat, he was twelve when the Nazis took over Danzig; later he became a member of the Hitler Youth. At seventeen he was drafted, was wounded the following year, and relatively fortunate, was taken prisoner by the Americans. Released in 1946, he tried his hand at various jobs, then became a student of art, particularly of sculpture. Around 1955 he emerged as a promising writer; four years later *The Tin Drum* made him famous.

Strikingly original though they are, Grass's works are indebted to many literary predecessors. He has mentioned Döblin, Unamuno, Büchner, Kleist, Melville, and Jean Paul, among others. I would venture the guess that he learned also from Grimmelshausen, Joyce (at least through Döblin), and Thomas Mann.

The Tin Drum

It would be pointless to tell again about the career of the gifted dwarf Oskar Matzerath before, during, and after the Second World War. *The Tin Drum* has been called a picaresque novel, a *Bildungsroman*, and sheer pornography. In a famous account of modern German literature, Grass's style is described as "naturalistic . . . with an alloy of surrealist gags," and as "the attempt at a 'black' literature in Germany."[3] I should like to approach his novels primarily as satires and to begin by considering *The Tin Drum* from the points of view of folklore, myth, and above all of literature. Certainly it is a work of linguistic art—*ein sprachliches Kunstwerk.*

Oskar's small stature is so obvious that one inevitably thinks of dwarfs—in Wagner, in Wilhelm Hauff's *Zwergnase*, in Ernst Barlach's *Der tote Tag*, and above all in Germanic folklore. Of course Oskar claims to have become a dwarf through his own voluntary act, and later he does grow a bit, though he becomes only a very small hunchback; he does not seem to want to attain normality in an abnormal world.

By consulting the standard encyclopedia of German superstition,[4] one can learn quite a bit about dwarfs, kobolds, and drums, and some of it seems very relevant to Oskar. Dwarfs, one reads, are often as small as children of one, two, three, or four; they are grown-up at three years of age. While Oskar is atypical in having a youngish face and no beard, he does wear, in Grass's own drawing for the jacket, the characteristic pointed cap, and he has bright, shining eyes. Dwarfs are especially fond of music; they often play the drum; their voices, like those of kobolds, are usually piercing—*dünn und schreiend.* Since male dwarfs tend to want to beget children larger than themselves, they often seek the love of beautiful fully grown maidens, who sometimes comply gladly. (Oskar, we recall, is the presumable father of a normal son.) Drums, furthermore, are often used for exorcisms, and their sound may prophesy that war is imminent.

More significant than these details is the fact that dwarfs are very ambiguous creatures, often malicious, often beneficent. Some have the evil eye; some help with the housework. Above all, they are both inferior to normal humans and, as possessors of magic powers, superior to them. This conception of the dwarf seems very close to the concept of the artist familiar in German literature from Goethe's *Tasso* to the twentieth century.

Basically the grotesque gnome Oskar Matzerath is an artist, and as such, mainly a satirist. People cannot resist the magic rhythms of his drum: he has the impact of a bizarre Orpheus; his spell is more powerful, though less sinister, than that of the magician Cipolla in Thomas Mann's *Mario and the Magician.* Further, his own voice has telekinetic power. Especially when he is kept from playing his beloved drum, he lets loose with a voice

> that enabled me to sing in so high-pitched and sustained a vibrato, to sing-scream so piercingly that no one dared to take away the drum that was destroying his eardrums; for when the drum was taken away from me, I screamed, and when I screamed, valuable articles burst into bits: I had the gift of shattering glass with my singing.[5]

Thus Oskar cannot only enrapture the masses; he can destroy and sabotage, and often does. Sometimes he acts out of sheer mischief: he often indulges in satire for satire's sake. Yet in his major performances he destroys, or at least ridicules, the meretricious and corrupt. In a polemic against Irving Babbitt, H. L. Mencken once claimed that he could make out the chin of Calvin behind the beard of Plato. Is it too much to sense that behind the blue-eyed mask of Oskar is the half-concealed face of Günter Grass, the greatest German satirist of his generation, who did not hesitate to let loose his far-darting arrows against Bertolt Brecht himself? Not coincidentally, one of the major characters of *Dog Years* is a satiric artist too: Eddie Amsel, the creator of grotesque artifacts which serve as scarecrows.

Oskar's far-reaching voice makes one think of Apollo; and it should be no surprise that the dwarf combines, in his own scurrilous way, Apollonian and Dionysiac aspects. Needless to say, Grass's use of mythological allusions is not highfalutin. Neither is it obvious, but it is there. For one thing, a writer so steeped in Joyce's work and obviously familiar with Mann's would not be likely to eschew the employment of myth completely. Moreover, after Nietzsche's *The Birth of Tragedy*, it has become a cliché, at least in Germany, that the true artist or poet must possess both the classic clarity of Apollo and the intoxicating emotional appeal of Dionysus. In Apollo, Nietzsche symbolized absolute form; in Dionysus, the appeal to the unconscious, the anonymous element in man. Both can be dangerous. At one point we read that Oskar "negotiated simultaneously with his gods Dionysus and Apollo" (p. 323).

A destroyer of shams, conventions, or anything else that annoys him, Oskar Matzerath is pretty clearly a miniature Apollo. As we know from the *Iliad*, Apollo, when angry, is formidable indeed: he slaughters his victims from afar. No one understood this aspect of Apollonian art better than Thomas Mann, who took that god's emblems, the bow, the arrow, and the lyre, as his own. In his brief essay "Bilse and I" he admits that a writer inevitably wounds the humans he uses as models for his fiction, even though that may be very far from his intention: "The expression which strikes the mark [*Der treffende Ausdruck*] always gives the effect of hostility. The well-chosen word hurts." [6] Similarly, Oskar directs the music of his drum or his piercing voice against anyone who has incurred his anger or disapproval—whether a relative, a schoolteacher, or a particularly unpleasant Nazi. Only images of Jesus and the Dove prove invulnerable, but Oskar is annoyed, rather than religiously moved, by this circumstance.

His greatest feat, however, is a Dionysiac one. He refused to join the spectators in front of a grandstand where the Nazis are about to stage a political demonstration, for his friend Bebra has told him that "people like us"—artists, that is—belong *on* the grandstand, not in front of it. But typically, he approaches it from behind—seeing its seamy side, so to speak—and then takes advantage of his tiny stature to slip underneath the stand, drum and all. Here he deliberately sabotages the celebration by striking up "The Beautiful Blue Danube" from his hiding place. There is loud laughter; many of the spectators join in. The color blue suffuses the whole place, Grass tells us; the nationalistic songs of the brown shirts are driven away. When the Nazi leaders (Grass uses their actual names) approach the speakers' stand, Oskar strikes up even bluer music, a Charleston, "Jimmy the Tiger." All the spectators begin to dance; the occasion is ruined, from the Nazi point of view; but the squads of SA and SS men sent to look for socialist or communist saboteurs never suspect that a whistling three-year-old child is the culprit.

Since Oskar's drum is apparently only a toy, few people take it seriously: he is an artist among Philistines. Yet it does attract attention. Ironically, Hitler, the invisible villain of the novel whom Grass alludes to as "Heaven's gas man" (one thinks of Eugene O'Neill's iceman) was known for years before he came to power as *der Trommler*—the drummer. In Oskar's hands, the drum loses its military aura and becomes an instrument for producing hot jazz—"Jimmy the Tiger" and so on—first in Danzig, then at the time after the war when Oskar becomes a member of the

Rhine River Three, a trio playing in a Düsseldorf night club.

To return briefly to the mythical level: Oskar is associated also with Hermes, the god of rogues. The dwarf functions as a picaresque hero or antihero as well as a satirist. Like Hermes, he can be mischievous, even malicious, but he is not really malignant. He refers to himself as "the little demigod of the thieves" (p. 130) and says elsewhere that Mercury blessed him. Like his literary ancestor Felix Krull, he has the strongly phallic aspect attributed to Mercury.

A few further points may help to establish Oskar as an artist. In his account of how he kept the grown-ups from interfering with his playing, he uses the technical term for aesthetic distance—*Distanz.* Late in the book, he meets a model whom he calls his muse. He has a strong affinity with the painter Lankes, whom he met during the war. Both of them are concerned to transform their harsh experience "into the pure, tinkling gold of the postwar period" (p. 551): the artist must live.

Whatever his vices, Oskar's cynicism is not central in his character: he is basically concerned with finding and expressing the truth. We recall that, at the age of three, he deliberately arranged the accident which made him a dwarf for life—or so he claims. Better to remain an outsider, a grotesque cripple, than to grow into a Philistine or a Nazi. In fact, there is a hint that Oskar's eventual hospitalization corresponds to his own preference: he would rather retreat into a metaphorical hermit's cell than be involved in the teeming but to him boring activity of the Federal Republic; he finds the atmosphere of postwar West Germany "Biedermeier."

Oskar's acquaintance Lankes characterizes the mood of the Nazi years as "mystic, barbaric, bored" (p. 337). The dwarf himself disclaims any connection with the resistance or the so-called inner emigration. To be sure, he helps a gang of adolescents perform acts of sabotage in Danzig during a blackout, but this is not presented as political activity. Oskar says expressly that he had aesthetic reasons for opposition: he disliked the color and cut of Nazi uniforms, and the music the Nazis played. In *The Tin Drum* the satiric tone is largely comic, at least on the surface. Fiercer attacks were reserved for Grass's second novel, *Dog Years.* Yet Oskar scores sharply when he describes a Rhinelander who always "screamed, laughed, and clapped" when others did (p. 152), and accordingly became a Nazi out of sheer conformism. When Oskar refers to a German cannon as "a virgin of the clan of Krupp" (p. 232), one is reminded of Erich Kästner's line "Kennst du das Land, wo die Kanonen blühn?" (Do you know the land where the cannons bloom?).

To turn to *The Tin Drum* as a verbal work of art: one may best characterize it, I believe, as baroque. This long, rich book is full of the violent contrasts, the extreme tensions which we generally ascribe to that style. Thus Oskar associates himself, as Erhard Friedrichsmayer has shown, with the infant Jesus, in a more or less blasphemous parody.[7] While there are scenes and images of great beauty —like the evocation of the January night in the chapter "Show Windows"—the language inevitably tends toward the grotesque. Of course Oskar's presence alone would account for that; his love affairs are particularly bizarre. Grass is addicted to picturing eels in a remarkably repulsive way, and his descriptions of vomit are almost literally emetic. His sense of death and underlying evil resembles that of the seventeenth century or the late Middle Ages. At the very end of the book, a sinister black cook is evoked;

she seems to symbolize guilt and may remind us of the black spider in Jeremias Gotthelf's novella of that name. For all his sense of comedy and wit, Oskar is whistling—or rather drumming—in the dark.

To continue on a more cheerful note: one observes that Grass has a sheer joy in words, which is comparable to Rabelais's or Joyce's—or, for that matter, to Heimito von Doderer's. Doderer is the more pleasant—at his best he is delightful—Grass the more "far-out," radical, and incisive, though at least one of the symbols (the octopus) in Doderer's *The Demons* is drastic enough to have been created by Grass.

A striking example of Grass's verbal gusto occurs in his description of the impact of the German bombardment on the defenders of the Danzig post office:

> There came a whirring as of angels' wings, a singing as of the ether singing over the radio. It didn't hit Bronski, no, it hit Kobyella, Lord, what a sense of humor that projectile had: bricks laughed themselves into splinters and splinters into dust, plaster turned into flour, wood found its ax, the whole silly nursery hopped on one foot [pp. 233–234].

He operates here with great skill, achieving his effect by cumulative parallelism and alliteration.

As one might expect, Grass delights in playing with words. Describing an imaginary geometrical figure which came to his mind while looking at a snapshot, Oskar relates, "I looked for a point, believing in points, addicted to points, a point of vantage, a point of departure, a standpoint" (p. 55). The use of two contrasting modes of narration—third person as well as first—also adds to the richness of the novel.

Symbolic images abound. The Nazi grandstand, hollow,

completely unimpressive once one gets behind it, comes to mind. When the hopelessly outnumbered Poles are surrounded in the Danzig post office, one of them builds an elaborate house of cards. Oskar's curiously mixed nature is illustrated by his two favorite books: Goethe's *The Elective Affinities* and a thriller about Rasputin. During the war, Oskar and other members of a troupe of performers, organized to entertain the *Wehrmacht*, act out an absurd little drama with soldiers guarding the Atlantic Wall in Normandy. It is the eve of the invasion, and concrete bunkers are everywhere, but the soldiers have had enough of martial life, of mysticism, barbarism, and boredom. Already they are dreaming of the prosperous Biedermeier period after the war, complete with bowling alleys, turtledoves, and refrigerators.

One other tension should be mentioned: that between a cynicism extraordinary even in our day and a certain paradoxical faith in man—an absurd humanism if you will. (Perhaps some day someone will note an analogy between *The Tin Drum* and *Doctor Faustus,* though this would probably annoy the revered shade of Thomas Mann.) There is no point in amassing examples of Grass's cynical wit: as the heroine of an English novel of the twenties said of Wagner's leitmotifs, you can't miss them. Quite aside from the erotic bits and the association of Oskar with Jesus, there are dozens of touches like the remark about the pieces of stone from bombed-out buildings which were "resurrected," as Grass puts it, to mark the graves of the dead—"if one can say such a thing about gravestones" (p. 544); or the designation of homosexuals as the "male girl-friends" of their protectors (p. 523). Yet the humanistic note is still heard: Oskar admires Goethe, even though he realizes that the admiration would not have been mutual; and something tells him that the Nazis could never win the war, "even if they . . . occupied Alaska and Tibet, the Easter Islands and Jerusalem" (p. 241). He defines "human" (*menschlich*) as "childlike, inquisitive, many-leveled, amoral" (p. 91). His definition tells us a great deal about himself and about Grass's reasons for choosing a grotesque little drummer as his hero.

Although *The Tin Drum* is basically a satirical novel, it has another, in a sense tragic, aspect. There is much concern with guilt, with Oskar's loss of innocence, and with related themes. When he changes from a dwarf into a small hunchback, he realizes, perhaps even exaggerates, his responsibility for the deaths of his mother, of Jan Bronski, and of his putative father, Matzerath. As A. Leslie Willson has shown, three colors have great symbolic significance: white suggests innocence; red, blood and sin; black, guilt.[8] At the end of the novel, Oskar is no longer primarily the satiric genius and rogue, but a man heavily burdened by his past.

Cat and Mouse

In its title, *Cat and Mouse* (1961), Grass's novella recalls the cat-and-mouse situation typical of Kleist's dramas: the protagonist, like the Prince of Homburg, Alcmene, or the Marquise of O——, is cruelly played with by a stronger power (or person), though he may eventually fight his way to salvation. Further, a central symbol of the novella is the Adam's apple of the protagonist, Joachim Mahlke, which happens to be exceptionally prominent. Now it is hardly a coincidence that the myth of Adam and Eve also plays a great part in Kleist's writing and thought, as in *The Broken Jug*, *Käthchen von Heilbronn*, and his important essay on marionettes. I believe that the interwoven, and typically Kleistian, motifs of cat and mouse and Adam's apple provide the key to Grass's story. In the first paragraph of *Cat and Mouse* one of his schoolfellows encourages a young cat to leap at Mahlke's twitching Adam's apple while he lies resting, apparently asleep, and the characteristic motifs recur consistently.

To turn to the action of the novella: it too is set at the time of the Second World War. Joachim Mahlke is an unusual youth, extremely brave, ambitious to a fault, and rather grotesque in appearance. He is tall and very thin, with an embarrassingly large Adam's apple. (There is said to be a belief among German schoolboys that this protuberance is an index to the sexual powers of its possessor. Although the actually highly sexed Mahlke is the most chaste of his group, the familiar association of apple, sin, and sex is clearly established.) In any case, his Adam's apple stamps the protagonist as a marked man. His extraordinary devotion to the Virgin Mary further sets him apart from his far from pious comrades.

Mahlke first demonstrates his bravery by feats of swimming and diving: he saves one boy from drowning. With his companions, he likes to spend time on the projecting deck of a small Polish warship sunk not far from Danzig. It is the "island" to which they escape from an irksome world, though their pastimes and conversation are not of the sort recorded in *The Swiss Family Robinson.* Mahlke is the only one who can dive well enough to penetrate inside the ship to a cabin which is still free of water. He makes it his shrine, and there he tries, perhaps, to take refuge from the army authorities at the end of the novella; the ending is deliberately ambiguous.

First, however, he has a military career of his own. It has an inauspicious background: Mahlke is disgraced for having stolen the decoration of a U-boat officer who was visiting his school. As this insigne—the Knight's Cross of the Iron Cross—is worn around the neck of its holder, it more than outbalances any Adam's apple, however unaesthetic, and irresistibly attracts the boy. Relegated to another *Gymnasium*, he soon volunteers for war service. With his tense devotion to duty, he manages to destroy so many Russian tanks that he is himself awarded the Knight's Cross. Returned to Danzig on leave, he is cruelly snubbed by the director of his original school, who refuses to let him address his former classmates, as the U-boat officer had done. This catalyzes Mahlke's discontent with society: he deliberately misses the troop train back to the front, beats up the director with the help of his friend and former classmate the narrator, and throws away his decoration. Hoping, or seeming to hope, to desert to a neutral country, he goes back with the narrator of the novella to the sunken ship. There he disappears and presumably dies. There is a strong hint of suicide.

Note that Grass has "distanced" the story by making a personal defeat, not some Nazi crime, the occasion of Mahlke's defection. It is nevertheless, I believe, a moral parable. Joachim Mahlke is a person of quite exceptional will power and courage. He also has more than his share of the "old Adam," but generally he keeps it in check: normally, he is downright ascetic. Here of course his devotion to the Virgin is relevant. His greatest strength—and weakness—is his extraordinarily competitive spirit. He focuses on performance as much as any of Mann's "heroes of creative work"—the *Leistungsethiker*. Typically, the appeal to competition is responsible for his only indulgence in one of the less attractive forms of adolescent sexual play.

An obscure sense of rivalry also leads him to steal the officer's decoration; characteristically, he confesses the theft voluntarily. Clear now about his own motives, he can win a cross of his own. In his eagerness to blot out his disgrace by appearing at his old school, he is abnormally sensitive: the director's refusal amounts to the end of his career. Fate or the era is playing a cat-and-mouse game with him.

Symbolically seen, the Knight's Cross represents to Mahlke a talisman, in fact a sort of "antiapple," which makes the embarrassing "apple" or "mouse" on his own throat irrelevant. When, however, he realizes that the way of life represented by that decoration is false, he throws it —and presumably his life—away. By so doing he saves his soul—to use an expression which Grass might find old-fashioned. Mahlke is the most admirable person in Grass's fiction, and the narrator—as Grass himself noted [9]—is impelled by a persistent guilt complex to write about his friend. We have no way of knowing whether the mouse Mahlke would have survived in a time when the cats were less cruel and vicious. There is one hint: he would have liked to be a clown, but the warlike mood of the period blocked that avenue of ambition.

Mentioning clowns reminds one that Oskar appears several times in *Cat and Mouse*, as does the unpleasant Tulla Pokriefke, who plays an important part in *Dog Years*. These carry-overs seem interesting and recall Grass's statement that he would like to devote a number of novels to the Danzig scene. Clearly, he is gifted enough to become the Balzac or Dickens of the former Free City. We should be grateful, however, that Grass also draws upon his experiences of the Rhineland and of Berlin. Fascinating though Danzig may be, it is hardly Paris or London.

Dog Years

Equally ambitious and almost equally long, *Dog Years* is darker in tone that *The Tin Drum.* It treats the same period, and most of its action takes place in the same areas: the territory of the Free City and the Rhineland. In fact, Oskar and his drum are mentioned several times. Its overall structure is more complex: there are three sections, each with its own narrator.

The other side of the coin is that *Dog Years* is less sharply focused than its predecessor. For one thing, the dog, or rather the succession of dogs, is not as potent a centralizing symbol as is Oskar with his drum—and with all respect for dogs, one must say that the dwarf is much more interesting than they. The second novel is harsher and less distanced than *The Tin Drum.* At times, the satire is heavy-handed, as in the account of the rumors circulated about Hitler's dog Prince after the Führer's inglorious demise. Yet *Dog Years* is a rewarding, many-faceted, and important book.

To deal first with the implications of the title: "Dog Years" seems to denote the period from about 1930 until some time after the close of the war. The third narrator, Matern, exclaims, "Oh, you hoarse-howled hound's years!" Possibly it is relevant that in the dog *days* men tend to be moon-struck, and dogs to go mad. Many or most of the generation Grass portrays are doglike in their blind, often stupid obedience. A poor wretch is an *armer Hund*, and *Du Hund!* is of course a crass insult. One may recall Erich Kästner's lines:

> Hier liegt ein Teil des Hunds begraben
> Auf den ein Volk gekommen ist—[10]

(Here lies buried part of that dog
To which a nation has gone.)

Hitler's weakness for German shepherd dogs is well known, and the Nazis were generally far kinder to animals than to people. When Harras, the father of the handsome dog which was given to Hitler, becomes vicious, Matern calls him Nazi.

The plot of *Dog Years* is basically simple: we read of boys growing up in and around Danzig, of the impact of Hitlerism and of the war, and of the postwar period. Perhaps the most interesting figure is Walter Matern, who protects his gifted, half-Jewish friend Eddie Amsel from bullies, but later betrays him. After the war, Matern, filled with guilt and anger, takes grotesque revenge on all the former Nazis he can reach. Amazingly enough, Eddie Amsel survives; his nickname in the third part is Gold Mouth: Nazi bullies, including his ambivalent friend Matern, have knocked all his teeth out.

The most striking aspect of the book is Grass's phenomenal virtuosity of style. Adroitly rotating his narrators, and repeatedly shifting the time of the narrative from around 1960 to the days before the war and back again, Grass revels in parody, puns, and other Joycean devices. His repeated parodies of Martin Heidegger are fierce but not, I think, unjust: the weird jargon of the Freiburg philosopher figures as a kind of double-talk which serves to conceal or evade reality. He is one of the former Nazis on whom Matern takes vengeance, calling him an "ontic dog," "pre-Socratic Nazi-Dog," and so on. These passages may seem senseless if one does not know Heidegger in the original; it is almost impossible to translate him into German, let alone into English. Thus the capitalized words "ICH, GRUND, GRÜNDEND IM ABGRUND!" lose much of their force when rendered as "I, ground, grounding in the abyss!"[11] Yet one gets the point when soldiers drafted by the Nazis parrot the sentence "The essence of being consists of its existence," when rats are described as "grounding in the ground," when the possiblity of a moonless night is expressed by the words "the moon, in case it should nothing" (*der Mond, falls er nichtete*), and so forth (pp. 298–300). In Grass's view, Heidegger has corrupted a language, which in turn served to corrupt its speakers.

Dog Years is full of bravura passages. Thus Grass compares the brown color of Nazi uniforms to dung and continues: "party brown, SA-brown, brown of all brown books, Brown Houses, Braunau brown, Eva Braun, this uniform-brown, far removed from khaki-brown" (p. 196). Twice, emulating Joyce, Grass constructs catalogues based on the alphabet, as for instance:

A as in "away with it" . . . B like "Bacchanal."—Now let us make merry. C like "Cato."—*Ceterum censeo*, we should kill another bottle. D as in "Danzig."—In the East it was prettier, but in the West it's better. E for "Eau de Cologne." —I tell you, the Russians guzzle it like rose water.[12]

And so on, and so forth. Some very rhythmical passages build up the effect of an incantation:

And the Vistula flows, and the mill mills, and the narrow-gauge railway runs, and the butter melts, and the milk gets thick—a bit of sugar on it—and the spoon stands in it, and the ferry boat comes, and the sun's gone, and the sun is there, and the sea-sand goes, and the sea licks sand [p. 54].

Elsewhere Grass imitates even the language of birds.

In a surrealistic radio forum, Walter Matern has to discuss his past with a group of young people who ask him very searching questions. The tone is deceptively light, parody and black humor abound, a chorus chants doggerel verses, but the essence is serious. One of the questioners has a pair of magic spectacles which reveal the past: Matern has no choice but to tell the truth. Although he claims to have been morally and politically pure, the sins of his dog years come out, including his part in the vicious beating of his friend Eddie Amsel by a Nazi gang. We learn also that he has slept with Hitler's mistress and that the black shepherd dog Pluto—to whom we must return—once belonged to Hitler. The point of this uncanny interlude would seem to be that the guilt of Matern's generation was all but universal. Since Matern loathes his past and tries in his confused way to atone for it, there is hope for him; but he must live with hideous memories.

Usually exuberant, sometimes excessively wordy, Grass's style can be concentrated and nervous. At times, to avoid banality, he breaks off a sentence before its end, leaving the reader to infer the rest. He describes a gypsy as follows: "A man middle forties. Pale brown black impudent, hidden behind the bush. Hook-nosed rabbit-eared toothless" (p. 95). Grass is indeed a man of many devices, and often his verbal arabesques and baroque flourishes obscure the narrative line.

Often fantastic though he is, Grass includes realistic, even naturalistic touches. To recreate the atmosphere of the Danzig region, he brings in local history, mythology, and superstitions. Frequently he has recourse to dialect. He names actual persons and firms: besides Heidegger he mentions Flick and other industrialists, Rudolf Augstein (the editor of *Der Spiegel*), Siemens and Halske, the Ullstein concern, and so on. At one point (p. 673), at least in some of the copies of the original, the name of a symphony orchestra has been inked out, presumably to avoid a law suit.

Yet, as in *The Tin Drum*, it is the major symbols which really take us to the heart of the matter. The first important one arises from Eddie Amsel's hobby of constructing grotesque scarecrows. (The descriptions of these weird artifacts remind one of some of Grass's drawings, such as that of the spider which illustrates his poem "Gleisdreieck.") Although Amsel's creations do actually frighten away the birds, they are essentially artistic renderings of his own experiences: he portrays in them people he has met and even records in scarecrow form an incident in which his schoolmates, already anti-Semitic, beat him cruelly. Surrealistic though these unusual mobiles are, they are based on nature: he feels that they are part of nature. Amsel's most important constructs, however, are images of SA men:

> Only Tulla and I knew he was making SA men who could march and salute, because they had a mechanism in their bellies. Sometimes we thought we could hear the mechanism. We felt our own bellies, looking for the mechanism inside us: Tulla had one [pp. 205–206].

(Compare Goethe's metaphor for Alba's soldiers, in *Egmont:* "machines in which a devil sits.") While the ordinary, obedient Germans appear as dogs, the Nazis are scarecrows, monsters. Amsel also plans to build a giant, phoenix-like bird which will always burn and give off sparks but never be consumed—a symbol of the creative artist, and perhaps of his own survival.

As the strength of the Nazi movement increases, in the second part of the story, so does the number of swastika flags along the Danzig waterfront. Eventually the war breaks out. The dog motif becomes more important: nasty little Tulla, so called after a mythical figure (Tulla's real name is Ursula), repeatedly sets the dog Harras on an inoffensive piano teacher. Prince, the puppy Harras has sired, is trained by the Danzig police and then presented to the Führer. For her part, Tulla, shocked by a swimming accident, regresses for a time into sheer animality: she spends a week in Harras' kennel, sleeping there and sharing his rations. Dog years indeed!

As has been mentioned, the third part of *Dog Years* is centered on Matern's adventures after the war and his determination to punish the Nazis he knew. Matern is all the more implacable because of his own guilt; in boyhood he was noted for grinding his teeth, and his temper remains fierce. Accompanied by the dog Pluto—the name is appropriate, for postwar Germany is seen as Hades—he travels over the countryside, exacting bizarre revenge from his victims. That he finds most of the culprits' addresses written on the walls of the men's room of the Cologne railway station is in line with the desperate sordidness of the first years after the German surrender. Matern's characteristic revenge is to debauch the wives or daughters of his guilty acquaintances.

The symbol of the prophetic meal worms—they live in a bag of flour belonging to Matern's father—is of a farcical sort. These worms can foretell the future, so leading industrialists and intellectuals make pilgrimages to the house of old miller Matern, who becomes more and more prosperous as the "economic miracle" continues. Finally the East Germans kidnap the remarkable little animals. All this may seem—or be—excessively farfetched, but I believe that Grass is satirizing a vein of superstition which still persists in Germany. Even otherwise intelligent people often turn to astrology, for instance.

The most successful symbol in Part III is the magic spectacles which play a decisive role in the radio program described above. These eyeglasses, produced in great quantity by the mineowner Brauxel—as Eddie Amsel now calls himself—enable young people to see exactly what their elders did in the Nazi years. Thus when the ten-year-old Walli sees Matern through the spectacles he has just bought her, she screams and runs away—and Matern is by no means the worst of his generation. Such eyeglasses are indeed easily available in Germany today—in accounts of the trials of Eichmann and other criminals, in movies, in dramas like *The Diary of Anne Frank* and *The Deputy*, and of course in innumerable books. The chasm between the generations could hardly be wider and deeper. It is a bitter but inevitable situation.

Appropriately, the long novel ends with a visit to Amsel-Brauxel's mine—the deep well of the past. The dog Pluto is taken down into the mine, but his name is not changed to Cerberus, for "Orcus is on earth," Amsel-Brauxel says, not beneath it (p. 561). The mine appears as a veritable inferno: Amsel-Brauxel is manufacturing scarecrows again, and his technique has become far more sophisticated. These automata are so processed that they can weep, laugh, hate, feel sexual emotion, and so on. They are indoctrinated in religion, military skills, and other knowledge—above all in German history. This reads like a dreadful indictment of all Germans, but Grass seems to exempt the younger, post-Nazi generation. Some readers have found his books "anti-German," but the genuine satirist pictures a society with which he is deeply involved: one thinks of Aristophanes, Juvenal, Swift, and Heine. No great satire against Hitler or Stalin has appeared, or is likely to appear.

The survivors are more or less reconciled; but memory and isolation remain. After emerging from the mine, each one takes a bath. Matern hears Eddie Amsel-Brauxel whistling in an adjoining cabin. To quote: "I try to whistle something similar. But it's difficult. We're both naked. Each of us bathes alone" (p. 561).

9/ A World Divided: Uwe Johnson's *Two Views*

"I would not say that any human life is banal."
—Uwe Johnson

"Today it is not enough to call a thing by its name; that has long since been corrupted. Now we must find new, valid names for things."
—Walter Maria Guggenheimer

Uwe Johnson's three major novels, *Speculations about Jakob* (1959), *The Third Book about Achim* (1961), and *Two Views* (1965), have in common the themes of alienation and frustration as exemplified by the division of Germany into two separate and increasingly disparate parts. Just as this division reached its sharpest and most striking expression in the building of the Berlin Wall, Johnson's portrayal of the Wall's impact on human beings is his most gripping book. Politics interests him primarily as it affects people; he seems to have little or no interest in governments and parties as such. Like Grass, Heinrich Böll, and Martin Walser, he is profoundly concerned with individuals and society here and now. Anything but a propagandist, Johnson is as keen a critic of life in the West as in the East; in fact at times he seems to lean over backward to preserve his objectivity.[1] Although he is sometimes referred to as a West German writer, this is misleading; he left the "German Democratic Republic" in 1959 but does not consider himself a refugee. As he has stated, he needs to live in the West in order to function freely as a writer but tries to write his books without partisanship, from a point of view located "on top of the Wall," as it were.[2]

Although all of Johnson's important work deals with the division of Germany and its effects and concomitants, he has not written the same book over and over; the style of *Two Views* is quite different from that of its predecessors. In *Speculations about Jakob* and *The Third Book about Achim* his style exemplifies in itself the uncertainties of perception in contemporary life, the almost insuperable difficulty of reaching the truth.[3] The reader can never be sure which conjectures about Jakob are correct, if any; and the third book, designed to tell the truth about Arnim, can never be written. Reading these novels fills one with admiration for Johnson's skill and his devotion to his moral and literary aims, and at the same time with a certain exasperation. Johnson's people in *Jakob* and *Achim* all move, blind or half-blind, in a post-Kafkan mist: after a while one gets the point all too clearly. Boredom threatens, as it does in the latter episodes of Kafka's *The Castle* and so often in the *nouveau roman.* Similarly, Johnson's linguistic devices for portraying the consciousness of his characters—interior monologues, violations of formal grammar, deliberately distorted punctuation, and so on—might well have hardened into mannerisms. In *Two Views,* he has surmounted both dangers. He still presents alienation but is much less likely to alienate the reader in the process: he must no longer grope his way in a labyrinth.[4] It is interesting to read that Johnson's first, still unpublished novel was rejected by publishers in East and West Germany; the latter found the story, though it showed great talent, unduly conventional.[5] *Two Views,* then, marks a third stage in his development: after his old-fashioned and his extremely experimental periods, it represents a middle way, but a highly original one. Since the author is still in his thirties (he was born in 1934), we may expect further changes.

Like Grass, Johnson seems to have concluded that there is nothing wrong in telling a story, even an interesting one. There is no lack of action in the "real" world he presents, as a glance at any Berlin newspaper makes painfully clear. In Johnson's latest book, as in the milieu surrounding it, there is nothing vague about an attempt to escape across a boundary. Whether or not Kafka's castle is real, there is no doubt about the Berlin Wall. Uncertainty and ambiguity arise less about what has happened than about the *why* and *how* in the motivations, the behavior, the misunderstandings of those concerned in the action. Thus Johnson's style in *Two Views* marks an advance in his presentation of contemporary society. As the title implies, he shows all the ambivalences of the scene; but at the same time his story has the old-fashioned attractions of suspense. Although we gather that nothing fatal will happen to D., the novel's heroine, during her flight, we become extremely tense while reading about it. Even that most primitive question, will boy get girl? plays its part.

Of course the style of *Two Views* is not really old-fashioned. Johnson is as painfully aware as before of the difficulties of finding and telling the truth; he has to wrestle with epistemology before sitting down to write. It is not only that Joyce, like Kafka, Broch, and others, "has enormously increased the difficulty of writing a novel." [6] The division of his country confronts a German writer, Johnson is convinced, with almost insuperable problems. To select one out of many incidents in his stories: in his "Eine Reise wegwohin, 1960" ("A Journey to Some Place or Other, 1960"), the fugitives from East Germany, arriving in a refugee center, find that they cannot communicate with the Western officials: "Here the East German language had fallen on evil days. It was not valid here; . . . its signals could not convey what they signalized." [7] (Johnson gives repeated evidence of linguistic sophistication.) In his essay "Berliner Stadtbahn," which appeared in English as "Border of the Divided World," [8] Johnson discusses the problems of the novelist in such a place and time. After noting that the Wall has created an enormous space between geographically adjacent buildings, he goes on: "A boundary in this place has the effect of a literary category. It requires us to change language and epic techniques to the point that they can cope with the unprecedented situation." [9] The two cities are "joined not by logic but by a frontier." [10] If a writer describes a man who has just crossed the border either as a refugee or as a deserter from socialism, he is taking sides; and he can hardly comment on the relative luxury of West Berlin without indicating approval or disapproval. He must avoid or "distance" himself from the official language of both factions. Above all, the author must admit his own handicaps and doubts, even if this involves the use of difficult and perhaps ineffective narrative techniques.

An excellent way of conveying this intention is to show two contrasting points of view, which is just what the title of Johnson's third novel implies. To call a novel *Two Views* suggests not only two views or opinions but two aspects: situations may differ objectively as well as subjectively. As a critic has suggested, the title may also be reminiscent of the German proverb to the effect that truth can be ascertained only by listening to the testimony of two witnesses.[11]

In fact, the structure of the novel is determined by the need for two viewpoints. Almost half of the story is told by a third-person narrator who follows the thoughts and doings of the young man B.; slightly more space is taken by the narrator's more sympathetic account of D., the girl. The two points of view alternate: a section devoted to B. is followed by one about D., of approximately the same length. Almost at the end, the first person singular suddenly appears. After B.'s accident we read, "I [the author, presumably] helped to pick him up;" [12] this touch gives an added sense of veracity. B. and D. are never seen together, although we hear of their brief meetings as lovers and of the girl's visit to B. in a hospital, at the end of the story.

In *Two Views* the use of initials for the main characters does not have the effect that the abbreviation K. has in *The Castle*. Rather than diminishing the reality or stature of the protagonists, the device adds a note of authenticity. It is as if the use of full names would violate security and make future escapes even more difficult than D.'s was. If this interpretation is correct, it represents a departure from neutrality on the narrator's part. In some situations, complete neutrality is impossible, and Johnson could hardly write as if millions of persons were eager to escape to the East at the same time that millions of others were demonstrably trying to go in the opposite direction. He balances things, however, by making the East German D. far more admirable and likable than her Western counterpart, who is a weak, dull fellow, but by no means evil; in his mediocrity and inadequacy he recalls Kafka's Josef K.

The action is simple and clear-cut, though some of the details and the motives remain enigmatic, in line with Johnson's convictions about the nature of perception. It begins in the summer of 1961, at about the time of the building of the Wall, and runs well into the following winter. B., apparently a rising young West German photographer, has had an affair with D., a nurse in an East Berlin hospital, in the days when it was easy to go from one sector of the city to the other. She loves him; he loves her—in his own fashion. After the Wall has been built, he manages to get a letter to her in which he proposes marriage and urges her to escape to the West. After some hesitation she decides to make the attempt. Largely by luck, he finds a group of admirable people engaged in smuggling refugees across the border. With the help of a counterfeit passport, they finally manage to effect D.'s escape. Arrived in West Berlin after her traumatic flight, D. finds that she no longer loves B. but decides to stay in Berlin; it is "her" city, however reduced.

Thanks to Johnson's combination of narrative methods, we get to know the two main figures in great depth. It is as if a very intelligent reporter were following first B., then D. with a camera and a tape recorder, and as if both of them, moreover, had confided many of their ideas, hopes, and worries to him. Thus the narrator knows D.'s thoughts when she is lying alone in bed, and even recounts four of her dreams. Yet this reporter is by no means omniscient: he has only "one view"; he tends to see events through the eyes of one or the other of the protagonists; it is the technique of *erlebte Rede*. When the proprietress of a Berlin bar looked over at B., we are told that she "laughed, perhaps good-humoredly." We can only infer her real feelings from the evidence of the novel as a whole. Yet although the reader has to remain alert, to judge or guess about certain matters, he has a far easier time with this book than with Johnson's earlier novels. There is no doubt, for instance, about when, how, and why D. crosses the border from East Germany to Denmark, though one of the most crucial factors affecting her escape remains unclear. In contrast, no one knows the circumstances surrounding Jakob's death or the reasons for it: it may have been a mere accident, but that seems unlikely.

B., the Western nonhero, is an "average sensual man"—actually a bit below average—reasonably intelligent but very insensitive. Quite immature for his twenty-five years, he has one great passion: sports cars. They are his leitmotif, his totem. The first sentence of the book states that he has purchased one; its theft seems to concern B. at least as much as does the separation from D. On the day she is to arrive in West Berlin—if all goes well—he is away, buying another flashy automobile. (In fairness it must be said that he telephones repeatedly and rushes back to the city the same evening.) He is particularly naïve about political matters, believing for instance that every Communist functionary is a model of absolute efficiency. He is not so much stupid as dreadfully imperceptive; his failure to remember the color of D.'s eyes, for example, gravely endangers her escape: the color is wrongly described on her synthetic passport. This failure—it seems—is the decisive factor in ending their relationship; she can no longer love him. During the time of their separation, disturbed by the apparent loss of D. (and of his car), he has begun to drink more and more compulsively. I doubt that either his materialism or his alcoholism is meant to be representative of the German Federal Republic: Johnson does not see things so simplistically. In a Communist country B.'s vices would be less expensive but not necessarily less serious. One can long as "materialistically" for an East German motorcycle as for a Mercedes Benz.

It is important to emphasize that B. is by no means a villain, any more than East Germany appears completely black. (There seems to be a certain contrapuntal symmetry here: B.'s weaknesses correspond to the darkness of the East, D.'s strength to the relative light of the West.) He has decent impulses, and he seems to be an imaginative as well as a competent photographer. Doubtless he loves D. as much as he can love anyone. He has told D. that he loves her; she is very much on his conscience, and he seems dimly to resent this. Basically he is an overage adolescent. Only this makes his callousness credible: the sum he is willing to spend for D.'s rescue is far less than the cost of a sports car. The narrator notes this twice, without comment.

On balance B. appears "other-directed," too much worried about other people's opinions. Above all, he is half-hearted, neither hot nor cold. He does not venture into East Berlin himself to try to rescue D., and the activists who play the role of the Scarlet Pimpernel seem to despise him. At the end he is severely chastised: D. refuses to speak to him; when she finally goes to see him in the hospital, it is a mere matter of form. (Appropriately enough, he has been injured, not too seriously, by an automobile.)

D. is a delightful person, recalling in some ways Brecht's Grusche in *The Caucasian Chalk Circle*. Unlike Grusche, she is no hero, and she suffers from a sense of inferiority: the East German state prevented her from completing her education, on the charge (quite possibly valid) that her father was a war criminal. She is a nurse, an appropriate vocation, for she is an *anima naturaliter Christiana*. By no means saintly, however, she has no qualms about lying to her supervisor about her trips to West Berlin, which were frowned on but not forbidden before the Wall went up. Typically, she smuggles Western medicines across the border as well as little luxuries for herself. The reactions of her patients and colleagues make clear that she is a person of integrity.

She is genuinely in love with B.: long after they have been separated, his "presence" pursues her. Nevertheless, she cannot completely trust him. Although several years younger than he, she is vastly the more mature and realistic of the two. When, after a few days and nights together, he declares that he loves her, she is vaguely embarrassed, presumably because of an unconscious distrust of his big words. Basically a loyal person, she maintains a certain faith in the East German state as long as that is psychologically possible. After she has decided to flee, she feels "cold from homesickness for the country which she wished to leave" (p. 211). A similar loyalty makes her refuse the chance to escape until the situation of her youngest brother has been clarified—and until she can be reasonably sure that B. is serious.

These conflicting pulls, added to her anxiety about the danger of attempting to cross the border, bring her to the verge of complete breakdown. Tortured by *Angst* and unconsciously by sexual deprivation, she tries unsuccessfully and very briefly to find solace in alcohol. Her dreams are horrible, and she comes to feel that she is two people: her real self and the automaton who carries on, very efficiently, with the day's work. Apparently she could not have survived the ordeal much longer. With good reason she is very much afraid of the East German *Apparat*, and she refuses any mode of flight which would involve shooting, but she manages to muster up the courage to cross the border with false papers. Precisely because she is rather timid, she cannot forgive B.'s carelessness in the matter of the counterfeited passport. (So at least it appears: Johnson leaves the reader to make his own analysis.)

A further complicating factor is that B. and D. have been educated to feel mutual hostility by their respective systems. She finds him politically naïve; he regards her society with a mixture of condescension, scorn, and superstitious fear. Thus each lover involuntarily hurts the other's feelings. D. is intimidated by "all these Westerners." *Two Views*, however, is not a sort of "Romeo and Juliet in Berlin," with the two German states cast as the Montagues and Capulets. If B. could have risen to D.'s level, things would have turned out very differently. By the same token, Johnson is not suggesting that "never the twain shall meet"; he is no determinist. B.'s failure as a person and as a lover is decisive. D. has not failed; she will remain in her native city. To quote the last sentence of the novel:

> She wanted to look at the extensive buildings . . . of the hospital before the visiting period was over, and in her overcoat pocket she had the weekend papers, fat with advertisements, job offers, and rooms to rent; she intended to find a room [pp. 242–243].

The two rival states do play an extremely important role, though not a decisive one. In fact they are almost characters, in the sense that time, in *The Magic Mountain*, influences the action nearly as much as any character does. Each sector is shown rather in its constant relation to the other than as an autonomous unit. Thus D.'s attitude toward East Germany is modified not only by the attractiveness of West Berlin shops, but equally by her annoyance with Western pretentions to superiority, a vague fear of life in a capitalist country, and so on. She cannot understand how the two half-cities can be so similar, in architecture for instance, and yet so different.

From what we see of it, life in the Federal Republic is a mixed blessing. From the point of view of D., imprisoned as she is, it is "the open world," yet she resents the "unfeeling comparisons" West Germans make between the two states. Further, they tend to make hypocritical declarations of solidarity with their unfortunate countrymen; a protest march in West Berlin is "half-hearted." The same word is used about B. himself (see pp. 129, 161). B.'s friends in the provincial town where he works seem excessively concerned with food, drink, sex, and money. Only the little group of rescuers B. meets in the bar is exempt, obviously, from any charge of indifference or materialism. (D. tends inevitably to see West Germany as B. writ large.) The description of Checkpoint Charley, of the tanks with their white stars drawn up on both sides, implies that to the politically impotent German observer, at least, there is no important difference between the two threatening powers. Since Johnson is not interested in writing a thriller or a tale of democratic heroes versus Stalinoid tyranny (which might well be true in itself), he keeps the "Pimpernels" in the background and includes another rescuer whose motive seems to be largely a financial one. Here the divergence between the two views is particularly crass: what is a gallant act from one point of view is officially described by the East German *Staatsmacht* as *Menschenhandel*, a word normally used to denote trade in slaves or prostitutes. (The unusual word *Staatsmacht* points up the state's obsession with its own authority.)

If Western society has a gray hue, life on the other side varies between gray and black. Of course it is the Wall which decisively darkens the picture. D. is driven step by step, largely against her will, to decide on "flight from the Republic." If she fails, she must face years in prison, and she feels guilty because her would-be rescuers are confronted by even greater risks. At first the injuries inflicted by the Eastern regime are relatively minor: she cannot continue at school, has to smuggle in medicines, must be continually on her guard against denunciation for petty political offences, and so on; but with discretion and some luck, she gets on reasonably well. The shabbiness of "her" country may be a function of socialist virtue, whereas Western prosperity is merely the result of American largesse, and the East Germans have at least atoned by their deprivations for Nazi crimes. (These are familiar propaganda themes, but even this "view" contains part of the truth.)

Once the Wall goes up, however, these arguments lose their force. So many people commit suicide that the morgues run out of room for their corpses; arrests become far more frequent; the secret police is now openly arrogant. When D. learns that one of the people who are working for her escape has been arrested, the impact on her is traumatic. There are hints that the East uses Nazi methods: it executes its coups on weekends as Hitler did; a worker is imprisoned for making a critical remark about the radical division of the city. In her fear of the dangers of attempted escape, D. thinks of "the dead, the wounded, in the canal, shot down by machine guns along the Wall, anesthetized by gas while hiding in drainpipes" (p. 196).

Res ipsa loquitur! Johnson's commitment to objective fairness makes his portrayal of the Eastern *Staatsmacht* all the more devastating. Yet Johnson, to his honor, never forgets the other aspect. As has been mentioned, D.'s venture is almost frustrated because of a gross error in her description on the counterfeit passport. Perhaps the agreeable official who should have noticed this was remarkably negligent or stupid, but there is no hint to that effect in the book. It is at least equally possible that he acted out of simple decency. The political import of *Two Views*, on balance, amounts to a condemnation both of the East German state and of the Western playboy type. In both cases, mitigating factors are fairly weighed.

Two Views is far more than a vivid, extraordinarily objective documentary novel about a political crisis. Johnson's style enables him to get under the skin of people as well as of states. I refer less to his skill as a narrator-observer than to the brilliance of his compact phrasing. When he describes a morning so gloomy that the street lamps had to be turned on, he uses a single adjective: *laternentrüb*. When B. had to walk the streets on a cold day, "he sensed nothing more than the quick, black wind which froze the sweat on his forehead into headaches" (p. 167). (If Johnson ever writes lyrics, they will be worth reading.) He refers to a branch of the West German intelligence service as "an office for the matter of questioning" —*Befragungswesen*—a word he seems to have coined. The account of the wardrobe furnished D. for her escape (she is to pass as an Austrian woman of the upper class) practically puts us in her borrowed shoes. Frightened though she is, the finery delights her; and the reader is led to admire the ingenious thoroughness of the Pimpernels who have provided her disguise.

Like his protagonist, Johnson is an expert photographer. He writes of "Christmas trees tied into great stacks near the white-blue light of the entrances to the subway" (p. 165), of the wards and nurses' quarters in the huge, mediocre polyclinic in East Berlin. He cites the renowned wit of the local taxi drivers: "Young man, your money is being ticked off on my clock" (p. 174).

Johnson uses symbols rather sparingly. B.'s sports car has already been mentioned; that the motor of his second racing automobile dies on the day of D.'s escape may be too pat. Of course the Wall, the fortified boundaries, and so forth, are so actual that it seems frivolous to speak of their metaphoric function. Stone walls do a prison make. Images of incarceration and escape pursue people into their dreams. Shortly before D.'s flight she has a nightmare about a secret subway system underlying the entire city. She has to crawl through tunnels, climb endless stairs, and above all, always keep going; but she never arrives. Obviously, this is a "frustration dream"; it also mirrors her awareness that hundreds of people tried and are still trying to get away through tunnels. The notion of a second, secret subway line suggests the desperate hope for another dimension, a sphere in which the reality of the present situation would not be decisive.

As in his earlier novels, Johnson tends in *Two Views* to use the style of colloquial speech with little regard for formal grammar and logic as such. A few rash critics have spoken of "mistakes" and "ignorance,"[13] but actually Johnson is attempting very consciously to find a style located as near as possible to the stream of consciousness.[14] His "relapse into parataxis," as Kolb calls it,[15] is part of this effort. The following sentence, monstrous though it might seem to many schoolteachers, is probably closer to the way most people speak and think than its "correct" form would be: "On the same day, I was just about to call home, I do hope my daughter is all right, I saw him, Cresspahl, for the first time."[16] Hugo Steger has shown in detail that Johnson's style is an oral one.[17] In *Two Views* he uses short, extremely direct sentences for the most part, but the paragraphs tend to run to several pages each. Paragraphing is often used to mark off clusters of associations rather than logical subdivisions.

Johnson is the antipode of Günter Grass: the two writers

complement each other neatly. In Johnson there is a preference for simple words, a certain tendency to understatement, a fidelity in reproducing ordinary speech, and an avoidance of effect for effect's sake, which may remind us of Fontane, despite all the obvious differences. Grass, at least equally as gifted as Johnson, revels in effects, in luxuriant verbal ornaments and devices of all sorts. Some of his finest scenes are wildly improbable, like the Tin Drummer's dispersal of a Nazi mass meeting, or completely visionary, like those of the automata in *Dog Years*.

As has been mentioned, Johnson uses the first person at the very end of *Two Views*, adding a note of authenticity. He is quick to qualify this, however. After D. has told him her story, she makes him promise not to repeat it: " 'But you must invent everything you write!' she said. It is an invention" (p. 242). Similarly, Goethe wrote of *The Elective Affinities:* "There is nothing in the book which was not experienced, but nothing is described *as* it was experienced." [18] Johnson's novel is a fictional metaphor of reality, and a strikingly convincing one.

Which of the "two views" is more nearly correct is left for the reader to decide. One point seems clear: whereas in the East the individual is endangered both from within and from without—by the system, the *Staatsmacht*—the terrors in the West are "not of Germany, but of the soul." Johnson is not suggesting that people are more virtuous and less materialistic when a tyrannical state keeps them in a state of enforced poverty. Rather, the corruption of B. (the word may be a bit too severe) indicates that freedom and prosperity—which is potentially a form of freedom—may indeed be perils for the weak. They are no threat to D. On the contrary, the fact that she has seen the strength and weakness of both views and has made her excruciatingly difficult choice is the foundation of her strength.

Johnson's success, especially in *Two Views*, affords further evidence—if more is needed—that the novel is not dead. When gifted authors find a major theme, great novels are likely to emerge, whatever the difficulties involved in writing them. It is high time that critics got away from mournful Spenglerite generalizations and got on with the job at hand.

10 / The Magic Square: Thomas Mann's *Doctor Faustus*

> "This style, this technique, he said, did not admit a single tone which did not perform its motivic function within the structure as a whole; there was no longer a free note."
>
> —*Doctor Faustus*

Soon after the appearance of *Doctor Faustus*, in 1947, critics began to sense that this was a work of extraordinary complexity, a controlled complexity in which a bewildering number of themes and episodes were arranged, on various levels, in accordance with a grand design. It was at once evident that more than one story was being told: the personal, musical, and political planes are interdependent yet distinct. It was equally clear that certain themes—the breakthrough, sickness, lateness, and so on—function on the various levels and link the planes together. The novel itself contains several hints that there is a strict basic pattern according to which everything has been ordered. Among other devices, the "magic square" and the twelve-tone system are used as metaphors for this pattern.

Of all the earlier interpreters of the novel, Victor A. Oswald, Jr., showed the most acute awareness of the book's structure. In three brilliant, brief articles, he provided startling insights into a few of its complications and enigmas, all of them important.[1] Mr. Oswald did not attempt to describe fully the novel's structure as a whole—that would have been impossible at the time he wrote and may still be impossible—but he had the clear and correct intuition that *Doctor Faustus is* actually a "magic square"; there is no "free note." More recently, Gunilla Bergsten devoted a scholarly and ingenious book to the sources and structure of *Doctor Faustus.*[2] Naturally it is less difficult to trace the raw materials Mann used in making his vast montage[3] than to give a fully adequate analysis of the principles he followed. Yet in pursuing hints given in earlier criticism that "The Lamentation of Doctor Faustus," the last work of the composer Adrian Leverkühn, may contain the key to the novel as a whole, she demonstrated that it does indeed furnish *one* of the keys.

Other hypotheses have also been suggested. Since the book "really" has forty-nine chapters—they are numbered one to forty-seven, but chapter xxxiv consists of three long sections—it was natural to suspect that Mann was again using his favorite numeral, seven, in his organizational scheme. (Seven is important in three of his earlier works, especially in *The Magic Mountain.*) J. Krey made the plausible suggestion that *Doctor Faustus* consists of seven books, each with seven chapters;[4] but this has been convincingly refuted.[5] Eva Schaper implies that the novel has five major planes of reference: the autobiographical, the historical, that of the "artist novel," the musical, and the Faustian.[6] In a confused but at times perceptive essay, Jon Tuska maintains that there are six levels.[7]

My own, very tentative hypothesis is that the "magic" number seven is indeed involved, but not importantly, in dividing the book into groups of chapters.[8] Rather, using the hints given by the magic square and the twelve-tone system, one should envision its structure both vertically and horizontally. In other words, I suggest that there are seven major themes, or clusters of themes, each of which is operative on seven levels. This assumption corresponds to the definition of the magic square: a group of numbers arranged in a square in such a way that they add up to the same sum, vertically, horizontally, and diagonally. The most appropriate example is the square pictured in Dürer's "Melencolia I," which itself figures in the book. Further, my notion fits Mann's analysis of twelve-tone composition, given in the novel itself.[9] The same notes, in the same order, are varied both vertically and horizontally in atonal music.

16	3	2	13
5	10	11	8
9	6	7	12
4	15	14	1

Of course it is notorious that an interpreter can be so intoxicated by his own theory that he unconsciously manipulates the data to fit it. "One can prove anything." Persons who know *Doctor Faustus* well can easily judge how much objective value my idea has. In some cases, the terms used may seem arbitrary: what I call the "salvation/damnation" theme could equally well be described as the motif of the "hellish pact." Often, though, the words and phrases used are clearly given or suggested in the book: the "breakthrough," the "end," the political and the Faustian levels.[10] Also, even if my hypothesis is valid, its correctness would not in itself make *Doctor Faustus* more—or less—interesting and important. Rather, since it is a work of great power and fascination, any suggestion which helps to clarify its structure, and thus perhaps its meaning, should be of some value.

The seven basic themes are intimately interconnected. Naturally, there must be interrelations among the several themes and levels, or the result would be chaos. Thus, "breakthrough" is intrinsically related to "salvation," to "expressivity," and so on; the various levels often touch and occasionally overlap: music, for example, is not totally cut off from either theology or politics.

Themes:

I. Breakthrough versus stagnation, cultural lateness —in Spengler's sense of the term—parody.

II. Hope versus despair. (Variations: rebirth and praise versus anxiety, lamentation, nothingness.)

III. Salvation versus damnation. (Variations: the angel [Echo] [11] and grace versus the devil figures or the pact.)

IV. Health (sanity) versus sickness (madness).[12]

V. Heat (or warmth) versus coldness (often symbolized in Adrian Leverkühn's laughter) and hubris.

VI. Humanism (exemplified by Zeitblom, but also by Goethe) versus barbarism, archaism (as in the use of sixteenth-century German), demonism.

VII. Expressivity versus control *or* sterility (or the beneficent variation of sterility, silence).

It is appropriate to Mann's dialectical form of thinking to take each theme as a polar duality. At times the "polarities" are united, as when Adrian's strictly controlled form results, in "The Lamentation of Doctor Faustus," in maximum expressivity.

Levels:

1. The Faust legend, especially as found in the early "Faust books" and in Goethe.
2. Music and, by implication, the other arts.
3. Politics.
4. Reminiscences of Nietzsche and other more or less Faustian figures (Dürer,[13] Beethoven,[14] Adrian Leverkühn's father, and so on).
5. Leverkühn's life.
6. Autobiographical references and concealed allusions to the novel itself.
7. Religion and theology.

If one takes the theme "breakthrough/stagnation" as an example, it clearly seems to apply, taking the seven planes in the order given above,[15] to the Faust legend, Adrian's music, Germany's attempt to "break through" to world power in the two great wars, the efforts of Nietzsche or Beethoven to find new modes of thought or music, the attempt of Leverkühn to break out of his isolation, Mann's own ambitions in writing *Doctor Faustus*, and the theological hope of attaining grace through the utmost contrition. It is examplified by the reference to Kleist's essay on marionettes, which argues that a man can be saved only by passing through a crisis ("going through an infinite [experience]") and by Mann's very free use, often amounting almost to direct quotation, of Theodor Adorno's dialectical philosophy of music.[16] Similarly, "coldness" figures on every plane, as in the cruelty of the archaic ideals enounced by the "Kridwiss circle," the isolated nature of Leverkühn's (or Nietzsche's) life, the sterility of parodistic art, and so on.

As has been noted, the magic square and the twelve-tone

system are metaphors for the structure of this novel. As such, they should not be taken too literally. The former seems more precise, for the action on every level does seem to "add up" to much the same desperate effort to emerge from stagnation, even at the cost of indelible guilt, and to achieve the breakthrough. Yet obviously some of the aims are legitimate, others not. The political thrust fails; the musical effort succeeds; for Leverkühn's salvation there is only "the hope beyond hopelessness," not the betrayal of despair but its transcendence. And *Doctor Faustus* is not a strict twelve- or seven-tone composition, but the brilliantly realized semblance of such a composition. Were it really a Schönbergian structure in words, no note (theme) would be more important than any other, and no theme could be sounded again until all the others had first been heard.[17] Such a structure may be theoretically possible, but a careful analysis of various chapters has convinced me that it is not the case. There is at least one convincing reason for this: *Doctor Faustus* is not a mere tonal pattern existing in time but has a large historical element, which of course involves time in a different sense. Thus, as in the legend, the themes of damnation/salvation and despair/hope occur with far greater frequency and force toward the end of the work than elsewhere. Further, Mann's artistic instinct, as well as his conscious virtuosity, inevitably kept him from slavishly translating musical techniques into literary ones. Yet it is true that there is "no free note": for example, the lyrics Leverkühn sets to music all have an intrinsic relation to his own life. Even the apparently trivial circumstance that Adrian stays at the house of a Signor Manardi in Palestrina (where Mann himself stayed) is part of the magic square. As Oswald has shown, Manardi was the name of a "precursor of modern syphilology."[18]

As one would expect, the most important chapters—xvi (Leverkühn in the Leipzig brothel), xxv (the dialogue with the Devil), and xlvii (actually xlix, Leverkühn's farewell to his friends and his collapse)—are most abundantly orchestrated; in each, all the levels and, with one possible exception, all the themes occur. In chapter xvi the breakthrough theme is not explicitly sounded; it would be premature, for Adrian has not yet "signed" the fatal pact; that is, he has not become infected. Yet to anyone who knows the novel, the theme is implicitly stated in the name Hetaera Esmeralda. A person reading *Doctor Faustus* for the first time will hardly be interested in such technical matters anyway—a point I shall return to. The dialogue with the Devil is naturally much concerned with the themes of warmth versus coldness, expressivity versus sterility, and breakthrough versus stagnation, which in this case largely coincide, and with the question of salvation or damnation. There is a great deal of political reference: the tortures of hell, where the unimaginable takes place, clearly derive from the "soundproofed cellars" of the Gestapo. In the last chapter (which includes the Afterword), the themes of damnation and salvation, despair and hope, predominate. The personal, religious, and political levels are foremost, and indeed almost fuse: Germany, like Adrian Leverkühn, is falling into the abyss, "in the grasp of demons, . . . God be gracious to your poor soul, my friend, my fatherland."

It may be helpful to indicate the succession of themes and levels in two important chapters. In the first chapter, the themes of hope/despair, humanism/demonism, and salvation/damnation (II, VI, and III) are stated on the second page. Themes VI, III, VI, IV (health/sickness), and V (warmth/coldness) follow in that order. Turning to the levels of the action, we find that the account of Leverkühn's life (5) is expectedly present throughout. (Since Zeitblom subordinates his own existence entirely to Leverkühn's,[19] his account of himself also falls on this plane.) The musical, political, and theological levels (2, 3, and 7) occur before the end of the second page, at which point the political element again figures. After that, the succession is 2, 1 (the Faust legend), 6 (the word *Steigerung* [intensification, heightening] reminds us of Mann's fascination with that concept, especially in *The Magic Mountain*), 7, 2, and by implication 6 (autobiography), if the reader is reminded by the repeated stress on coldness of the frequently laid charge that Mann's own work and personality were cold. This reproach particularly concerned him when he was a young man. (See his letters to Katja Pringsheim during their engagement,[20] and the problem of the hero's coldness in *Royal Highness*.)

In the climactic chapter xxv, in which the dialogue with the Devil is preceded by Zeitblom's brief, horrified introduction, we encounter the various themes in the following order: IV, III, VII (expressivity/silence), III, V, III, V, III, IV, III, V, III, VII, IV, III, IV, VII, III, VII, I, III, IV, VII, IV, VI, III, IV, V, III, I, V, IV, III, IV, I, VI, I, IV, I, IV, VI, II, III, II, V, III, V, II, V, I, V, IV, III, V. As has already been noted, health, salvation, expressivity, and coldness, with their opposites, predominate. The relatively infrequent and late appearance of Theme II (hope versus despair) derives from the fact that Leverkühn does not begin really to worry about the terms of the pact and seek for a way of escaping them until near the end of the dialogue. It takes some time for him to sense that this multivisaged devil (who appears in a variety of shapes) is in a profound sense real.

A list of the various levels of reference, in the order of their appearance, would be easy to supply but seems hardly necessary. Those which occur most frequently and are maintained the longest are, along with the biographical, the planes of music, theology, and politics. It is important to note that two or more levels may be simultaneously involved: thus the theological may coincide with the political, as when hell is identified with Nazi prisons. Of course, two or more themes can be sounded together to form a sort of chord: in Adrian's case, his illness—as the ground of his genius—comes to coincide with the breakthrough and with his probable damnation or possible salvation.

A chord of another type results when two or several strata of time are present at once. Mann gives a striking example in *The Story of a Novel: The Genesis of "Doctor Faustus"* of the way Zeitblom's reactions to the story he is relating are combined with the events occurring as he writes it down: "so that the trembling of his hand caused by the vibrations of bombs striking far away and by the horror within him is explained in two ways which nevertheless fuse into one." [21] As Zeitblom states that his account will be read, if at all, only after the fall of the German state, there is a third "time," the reader's. Further, a person who is aware that Leverkühn "is" Nietzsche in some instances and "is" the legendary Faust in others also experiences the "times" of the sixteenth and nineteenth centuries. By adding time as a dimension, Mann has in fact approached the pattern of a magic cube.

Birgit Nielsen convincingly presents a similar if more sophisticated argument.[22] After reminding us that Mann was fascinated by the idea of the "lived Vita"—a life consciously modeled on that of some great figure of the past—she shows that Leverkühn consciously imitates the career of the chapbook Faustus. (Similarly, Napoleon explicitly identified himself with Julius Caesar, Mann's Joseph with the gods who had died and risen again.) Miss Nielsen notes a host of correspondences between Adrian's career and those related to Faustus in the Spies version, and others, of the legend. As she freely concedes, most or all of these have already been pointed out. Her contribution is to make clear that Leverkühn, who obviously was well acquainted with the legend, deliberately followed in Faustus' footsteps.[23] At the end, Adrian Leverkühn's farewell to his friends in an *imitatio* of an *imitatio*. It is obviously modeled on Faustus' farewell speech to his students, which in turn recalls or parodies (in a sinister sense) Christ's last hours with the disciples. Faustus replaced the words "Watch with me!" by "Sleep calmly and let nothing disturb you!" As Zeitblom observes, Adrian feels the need for human beings around him, despite all his pride. Although he collapses into madness, like Nietzsche, his final gesture, with arms outstretched, suggests the Crucifixion. In Mann's view, there is a Christlike element in Leverkühn's sacrificing himself for the "breakthrough" of a new, genuinely expressive music.

Anyone who has followed the argument this far will very possibly wish to raise a familiar objection to Mann's novel: How can a work of such extreme complexity, such self-conscious elaboration, move the reader emotionally? Differently put: Mann tells us that Leverkühn's "Lamentation of Doctor Faustus" attained the greatest expressivity by use of the most exactly controlled techniques. But does not Mann fail where Leverkühn succeeded? (To repeat, "The Lamentation" is a cipher for the structure and the intention of *Doctor Faustus*.)[24]

The objection is a very natural one but not, I think, valid. In his article "Adrian Leverkühn as a Composer," J. M. Stein writes of the effect of twelve-tone music: "Since the ramifications of the twelve-tone discipline are so intricate, . . . it is impossible for the listener to experience the form during a performance."[25] Stein implies that the same argument applies to Mann's novel. In other words, a sympathetic reader of *Doctor Faustus* is subjected, in the more intense sections of the work, to a veritable barrage of emotional stimuli. In the "Lamentation" chapter, for instance, his feelings about the war, his reactions (positive, negative, or mixed) to the fate of Germany, and his empathy for Adrian Leverkühn are all involved, along with other, less central reactions; his emotions are evoked by a repeated and eloquent statement of the major themes. (Here, as in the other high points of the book, we hear Mann's or, in some cases, Leverkühn's voice, not Zeitblom's.) Expressivity has indeed been realized. This is Thomas Mann's breakthrough, his triumph.

NOTES

Chapter 1. The Renovation of the German Novel: Theodor Fontane

1. *Sämtliche Werke* (Munich: Nymphenburger Verlagshandlung, 1959——).

2. *Formen des Realismus: Theodor Fontane* (Munich: Hanser, 1964).

3. *Theodor Fontane* (Munich: Piper, 1967).

4. Aside from Fontane, the writers who made the greatest impact on the German novel in the late nineteenth century were non-German, primarily French, Russian, and Scandinavian.

5. See Joachim Remak, *The Gentle Critic: Theodor Fontane and German Politics, 1848–1898* (Syracuse, N.Y.: Syracuse University Press, 1964), p. 5.

6. *Briefe an Georg Friedlaender*, ed. K. Schreinert (Heidelberg: Quelle and Meyer, 1954), p. 131; see also p. 160.

7. Conrad Wandrey, *Theodor Fontane* (Munich: Beck, 1919), p. 216; see also *Briefe an Friedlaender*, p. xxi.

8. *Gesammelte Werke* (Berlin: F. Fontane, 1905–1910), Series 2, VI, 112 (hereafter cited as *G.W.*); quoted in Fritz Martini, *Deutsche Literatur im bürgerlichen Realismus* (Stuttgart: Metzler, 1962), p. 800.

9. *Briefe an Friedlaender*, p. 133.

10. *Reinterpretations* (London: Thames and Hudson, 1964), p. 341.

11. Remak, *Gentle Critic*, p. 41.

12. *Briefe an Friedlaender*, p. 283.

13. *Theodor Fontane*, pp. 27–33.

14. *Briefe an Friedlaender*, p. 147.

15. *Ibid.*, p. xxi. Cf. *G.W.*, Series 2, XI, 380.

16. Thomas Mann, *Gesammelte Werke* (Frankfort on the Main: S. Fischer, 1960), IX, 27.

17. Brinkmann, *Theodor Fontane*, p. 116.

18. *Ibid.*, p. 94.

19. *Briefe an Friedlaender*, p. 157.

20. *Ibid.*, p. 215.

21. *G.W.*, Series 2, VI, 231.

22. A term applied by Lionel Trilling to E. M. Forster in his well-known book on that novelist.

23. Fontane, *Schriften zur Literatur*, ed. H. H. Reuter (Berlin: Aufbau-Verlag, 1960), p. vii (hereafter cited as *Schriften*).

24. *G.W.*, Series 2, VII, 290–291; quoted by Brinkmann, *Theodor Fontane*, p. 112.

25. *Theodor Fontane*, p. 181.

26. See Georg Lukács, *Deutsche Literatur in zwei Jahrhunderten* (Neuwied and Berlin: Luchterhand, 1964), pp. 452–498, esp. pp. 456–457 and p. 468. The essay can also be found in Lukács' *Deutsche Realisten des 19. Jahrhunderts* (Berlin: Aufbau-Verlag, 1952).

27. Martini, *Deutsche Literatur im bürgerlichen Realismus*, p. 737.

28. Demetz, *Formen des Realismus*, pp. 140–142.

29. To be sure, Czako may have chosen the theme in order to descend to the level of his very earthy dinner partner, Frau von Gundermann, but even Stechlin does not find the topic unappetizing.

30. Martini, *Deutsche Literatur im bürgerlichen Realismus*, p. 769.

31. Wandrey, *Theodor Fontane*, p. 195.

32. *Formen des Realismus*, p. 179.

33. Percy Lubbock, *The Craft of Fiction* (London: Cape, 1963), pp. 71, 83, *et passim.*

34. Quoted by Mann, *Gesammelte Werke*, IX, 21.

35. Demetz, *Formen des Realismus*, p. 179.
36. *Schriften*, p. 98.
37. Mann, *Gesammelte Werke*, IX, 23.
38. *Ibid.*
39. *G.W.*, Series 2, XI, 418, letter of Feb. 14, 1897.
40. *Formen des Realismus*, p. 134.
41. Wandrey, *Theodor Fontane*, p. 252.
42. *The Structure of the Novel* (London: Hogarth, 1963), pp. 25–26.
43. P. 174. Page references are to *G.W.*, Series 1, VIII.
44. Wandrey, *Theodor Fontane*, p. 252.
45. *Schriften*, p. 320.
46. Wandrey, *Theodor Fontane*, p. 278.
47. See Marianne Bonwit, "Effi Briest und ihre Vorgängerinnen . . . ," *Monatshefte*, XL (1948), 445–456; H. Geffcken, "Effi Briest und Madame Bovary, *Das literarische Echo*, XXIII (1921), cols. 523–527; J. P. Stern, *Reinterpretations*, pp. 316–339; and Friedrich Spielhagen, *Neue Beiträge zur Theorie und Technik der Epik und Dramatik* (Leipzig: Staackmann, 1898), pp. 91–122.
48. P. 164. Quotations from *Effi Briest* and *Der Stechlin* are from *G.W.*, Series 1, vols. IX and X, respectively.
49. Wandrey, *Theodor Fontane*, p. 273.
50. Demetz, *Formen des Realismus*, pp. 204–216.
51. Cf. Mary E. Gilbert, "Fontanes Effi Briest," *Der Deutschunterricht*, XI (1959), No. 4, p. 66.
52. One is reminded of Goethe's characterization through repeated (and mutual) mirrorings—*wiederholte Spiegelungen.*
53. Cf. Wandrey, *Theodor Fontane*, p. 280.
54. Cf. Geffcken, "Effi Briest und Madame Bovary."
55. Spielhagen, *Neue Beiträge*, p. 109.
56. *Schriften*, p. 174; cf. Gilbert, p. 68.
57. *Schriften*, p. 321.
58. Cf. Lukács, *Deutsche Literatur*, pp. 452–498, esp. p. 497.
59. See Julius Petersen, "Fontanes Altersroman," *Euphorion*, XXIX (1928), 2–3.

60. See Walter Müller-Seidel, "Der Stechlin," in *Der deutsche Roman*, ed. B. von Wiese (Düsseldorf: Bagel, 1963), II, 180.

61. Erich Behrend, *Fontanes "Stechlin"* (Marburg: Elwert, 1929), pp. 60–61.

62. Letter to C. R. Lessing, June 8, 1896, *G.W.*, Series 2, XI, 388.

63. Petersen, "Fontanes Altersroman," p. 49.

64. To conceal the identity of the "original Effi" who was alive and active when the book appeared, Fontane found it necessary to have his heroine die (*Schriften*, p. 322). His chivalry exacted a high price, for the last section of the book is by far the weakest.

65. *Briefe an Friedrich Paulsen* (Bern: Dürr, 1949), p. 5, letter of Nov. 29, 1897.

66. See Petersen, "Fontanes Altersroman," p. 44; and Behrend, *Fontanes "Stechlin,"* p. 39.

67. Behrend, *Fontanes "Stechlin,"* pp. 63–64.

68. Cf. *ibid.*, p. 32.

69. Müller-Seidel, "Der Stechlin," p. 172.

Chapter 2. An Unsentimental Education: Robert Musil's *Young Törless*

1. *Die Verwirrungen des Zöglings Törless*, in Robert Musil, *Prosa, Dramen, Späte Briefe*, ed. Adolf Frisé (Hamburg: Rowohlt, 1957), esp. pp. 30–31. Page references in this chapter are to this edition; all translations are my own.

2. Quoted in Robert Minder, *Kultur und Literatur in Deutschland und Frankreich* (Frankfort on the Main: Insel-Verlag, 1962), p. 81.

3. The reactionary, pseudoromantic character of Fascism was often stressed by Thomas Mann, especially in *Doctor Faustus*.

4. *Kultur und Literatur*, p. 83.

5. There were *two* secret rooms in the cellar of the South

German *Realgymnasium* I attended in 1926: the "victory chamber" and the "death chamber."

6. At one point, apparently inadvertently, the narrator calls himself "I" (p. 17).

7. "A Short View of Musil," *Encounter*, XV (Dec., 1960), 64.

8. Ulrich Karthaus, "Musil-Forschung und Musil-Deutung," *Deutsche Vierteljahresschrift . . .*, XXXIX (1965), 463.

9. *Robert Musil: An Introduction to His Work* (Ithaca: Cornell University Press, 1961), p. 43.

10. "Les Désarrois de l'élève Törless, *Preuves*, X (Nov., 1960), 83.

11. See Ernst Kaiser and Eithne Wilkins, *Robert Musil: Eine Einführung in das Werk* (Stuttgart: Kohlhammer, 1962), p. 67.

12. "Yet a shadow falls from those lives / Over into the other lives, / And the light ones are bound to the heavy / As to air and earth" ("Manche freilich . . . ," in *Gedichte und Lyrische Dramen*, ed. Herbert Steiner [Stockholm: Bermann-Fischer, 1946], p. 20).

13. That the last sentence of the book refers to Törless' awareness of his mother's perfume is provocative. Although the theme of incest is important in Musil, this sentence, I think, serves primarily to point up Törless' new awareness of his mother as a sexually attractive human being; it should not be overinterpreted. See Minder, *Kultur und Literatur*, p. 84; Kaiser and Wilkins, *Robert Musil*, pp. 74–76.

14. *Gesammelte Werke* (Frankfort on the Main: S. Fischer, 1960), VIII, 288.

15. Pike, *Robert Musil*, p. 44.

Chapter 3. Life as Nightmare: Franz Kafka's "A Country Doctor"

1. *Beschreibung eines Kampfes* (Frankfort on the Main: S. Fischer, 1946), p. 96.

2. See Basil Busacca, "A Country Doctor," in *Franz Kafka*

Today, ed. A. Flores and H. Swander (Madison: University of Wisconsin Press, 1958), pp. 45–54; and Heinz Politzer, *Franz Kafka: Parable and Paradox* (Ithaca, N.Y.: Cornell University Press, 1962).

3. Busacca, "A Country Doctor," pp. 45–46.

4. "Zur Entstehungsgeschichte von Kafkas Landarzt," *Monatshefte*, XLVI (1954), 207–212.

5. See Kafka's "testament"—one of the two notes he sent Max Brod about the disposition of his books and manuscripts —quoted in Politzer, *Franz Kafka*, p. 295.

6. "Kleine Erinnerungen an Franz Kafka," quoted in Max Brod, *Franz Kafka: Eine Biographie* (Frankfort on the Main: S. Fischer, 1962), p. 332.

7. Through the use of "*erlebte Rede*" Kafka gives us the point of view of a character while using the third person. The opening sentence of *The Trial*—"Someone must have slandered Josef K., for although he had not done anything bad, he was arrested one morning"—gives us the protagonist's interpretation, not the comment of an omniscient narrator.

8. *The Frozen Sea* (New York: Oxford University Press, 1948), p. 80.

9. The text used is Franz Kafka, *Erzählungen und Kleine Prosa* (New York: Schoeken Books, 1946). In view of the extreme brevity of the story, no page references are given. The translation is my own.

10. I am grateful to Miss Sandra Shuman, who called my attention to this decisive point.

11. Cf. Helmut Motekat, in *Interpretationen moderner Prosa* (Frankfort on the Main, Berlin, Bonn: Diesterweg, 1956), p. 16.

12. Act II, "Egmonts Wohnung," J. W. Goethe, *Werke*, VIII (Weimar: Böhlau, 1889), 220.

13. See Klaus Wagenbach, *Franz Kafka: Eine Biographie seiner Jugend* (Bern: Francke, 1958), p. 259.

14. Thomas Mann, *Gesammelte Werke* (Frankfort on the Main: S. Fischer, 1960), VIII, 700.

15. See Herman Salinger, "More Light on Kafka's 'Landarzt,'" *Monatshefte*, LII (1961), 99; and Walter Sokel, *Franz Kafka: Tragik und Ironie* (Munich: Langenmüller, 1964), p. 259. Such references to psychoanalysis (and other nonliterary matters) frequently provide useful analogies, but not complete explanations.

16. I am indebted to Professor Bluma Goldstein for this information.

17. See the discussion of the doctor as a healer or savior, below. In the world of "A Country Doctor" true saviors do not exist.

18. See Wilhelm Emrich, *Franz Kafka* (Bonn: Athenäum, 1961), pp. 129–137, for a different interpretation.

19. Politzer, *Franz Kafka*, p. 347.

20. Sokel, *Franz Kafka*, p. 268; Bluma Goldstein, "A Study of the Wound in the Works of Franz Kafka," *Germanic Review*, XLI (1966), 202–217.

21. *Tagebücher*, ed. Max Brod (Frankfort on the Main: S. Fischer, 1951), p. 315, entry of Aug. 14, 1913.

22. "More Light on Kafka's 'Landarzt,'" pp. 100–102.

23. Albrecht, "Zur Entstehungsgeschichte von Kafkas Landarzt," p. 212.

24. See Richard H. Lawson, "Kafka's 'Der [*sic*] Landarzt,'" *Monatshefte*, IL (1957), 265–271. He suggests (p. 270) that the line "Freuet euch, ihr Patienten," may contain a pun on Freud; but Kafka's plays on words are much more rewarding than this. See also Eric Marson and Keith Leopold, "Kafka, Freud, and 'Ein Landarzt,'" *German Quarterly*, XXVII (1964), 160.

25. "A Country Doctor," p. 52.

26. Cf. Politzer, *Franz Kafka*, p. 89.

27. *Hochzeitsvorbereitungen auf dem Lande* (Frankfort on the Main: S. Fischer, 1953), p. 81.

28. Wolfdietrich Rasch uses this term to describe the ending of Goethe's *Torquato Tasso*. See Rasch, *Goethes Torquato Tasso* (Stuttgart: Metzler, 1954), p. 170.

Chapter 4. Accepting the Universe: Hermann Hesse's *Steppenwolf*

1. *The Lyrical Novel* (Princeton: Princeton University Press, 1963).

2. "Zur Erklärung von Hermann Hesses *Steppenwolf*," *Monatshefte*, LIII (1961), 198.

3. *Krisis* (Berlin: S. Fischer, 1928), p. 81.

4. Schwarz, "Zur Erklärung von Hermann Hesses *Steppenwolf*," pp. 192, 197.

5. Compare for instance Mann's phrase "problem child [*Sorgenkind*] of life" (my translation) and Hesse's use of the word *Sorgenkind* in *Der Steppenwolf* (Zurich: Manesse Verlag, n.d.), p. 37. Page numbers in the text refer to this edition; all translations are my own. The quotation from "The Immortals" is by permission of Suhrkamp Verlag.

6. *Krisis*, pp. 10–11; used by permission of Suhrkamp Verlag.

7. For a similar criticism of Goethe, see Erich Heller, "Goethe and the Avoidance of Tragedy," in his *The Disinherited Mind* (Philadelphia: Dufour and Saifer, 1952), pp. 27–49.

8. In "psychedelic" circles, it is claimed that Hesse took drugs; it has also been maintained that he was an "overt homosexual" (*New Republic*, July 13, 1968, p. 24). Doubtless these assertions will interest persons of certain persuasions; they have no literary relevance, and remind one of questions like "Was Shakespeare a sailor?" "Could Goethe swim?"

9. *Sämtliche Werke*, VI (Stuttgart: Kröner, 1965), 173.

10. See Malte Dahrendorf, "Hesses *Demian* und Jung," *Germanisch-Romanische Monatschrift*, XXXIX (1958), 89.

11. See Edward Glover, *Freud or Jung* (New York: Norton, 1950), esp. pp. 30–32, 61–62.

12. *Ibid.*, esp. pp. 187–195.

13. Schwarz, "Zur Erklärung von Hermann Hesses *Steppenwolf*," p. 193.

14. See Paul Roth, *Anima und Animus in der Psychologie C. G. Jungs* (Winterthur, Switz.: Keller, 1954), pp. 50–51.

15. See Theodore Ziolkowski, *The Novels of Hermann Hesse* (Princeton: Princeton University Press, 1965), pp. 178–228.

16. *The Lyrical Novel*, pp. 76–77.

17. *Ibid.*, pp. 78–79.

Chapter 5. Myth versus Secularism: Religion in Thomas Mann's *Joseph*

1. See *Mystik der Gottesferne* (Bern and Munich: Francke, 1960), *passim.*

2. See *The German Tradition in Literature, 1871–1945* (Cambridge: University Press, 1965), esp. pp. 105–223.

3. C. June 6, 1935; in Sigmund Freud, *Letters*, ed. Ernst L. Freud (New York: Basic Books, 1960), p. 426.

4. *Johann Wolfgang Goethe* (*Gedenkausgabe*), X (Zurich: Artemis, 1948), p. 157.

5. *Gesammelte Werke* (Frankfort on the Main: S. Fischer, 1960), X, 258–259. Volume and page references are to this edition. Translations are my own.

6. X, 267, *et passim.*

7. At the end of the novel—to disagree with one point while agreeing with the rest—Joseph does understand his own limitations, I believe.

8. "Joseph and His Brothers: A Comedy in Four Parts," in *The Happy Critic* (New York: Hill and Wang, 1961), p. 74.

9. IV, 39–49.

10. The fact that "spirit" is masculine and "soul" feminine in German is of psychological, mythical, and perhaps even philosophcial importance.

11. IV, 39.

12. Mann speaks of a "higher identity" of spirit and soul, and seems to hint that the future will make this clear.

13. Cf. Gray, *The German Tradition in Literature*, pp. 185–207, esp. p. 187.

14. IV, 43.

15. Gen. 50:26.

16. Also, since Mann calls *Geist* the "second ambassador," God must have intended the soul to behave as "she" did (IV, 42, 45–46).

17. *In the Clearing* (New York: Holt, Rinehart and Winston, 1962).

18. Käte Hamburger, *Der Humor bei Thomas Mann* (Munich: Nymphenburger Verlagshandlung, 1965), p. 203. This book is a revision of Frau Hamburger's *Thomas Manns Roman "Joseph und seine Brüder": Eine Einführung* (Stockholm: Berman-Fischer, 1945).

19. Cf. Hamburger, *Der Humor*, p. 200.

20. V, 1284.

21. V, 1287.

22. *Briefe, 1948–1955*, ed. Erika Mann (Frankfort on the Main: S. Fischer, 1965), pp. 231–232, letter to H. Hatfield, Nov. 19, 1951.

23. This brief story, not one of his major achievements, is briefly discussed below.

24. In *Die Entstehung des Doktor Faustus* (Amsterdam: S. Fischer, 1949), p. 20.

25. Exod. 31:18.

26. See Sigmund Freud, *Der Mann Moses und die monotheistische Religion* (1938) and Käte Hamburger's introduction to her edition of *Das Gesetz* (Frankfort on the Main: Ullstein, 1964).

27. VIII, 850.

28. VIII, 851.

29. VIII, 872.

30. VIII, 850.

31. VIII, 851.

32. VIII, 873.
33. VIII, 875.
34. *Der Humor*, p. 147.
35. *The Secular City* (New York and London: Macmillan, 1966), p. 72.
36. *The Enlightenment: An Interpretation*, I (New York: Knopf, 1966), 151.

Chapter 6. Vitality and Tradition: Two Novels by Heimito von Doderer

1. *Die Strudlhofstiege oder Melzer und die Tiefe der Jahre* (Munich: Biederstein Verlag, 1951). References in the text pertain to this edition. Translations are my own. "Auf die Strudlhofstiege zu Wien" is used by permission of Biederstein Verlag.
2. In a brief article, "Un Romancier autrichien de la décadence," on *Die Strudlhofstiege*, *Mercure de France*, CCCXX (1954), pp. 525–528.
3. There are references to Austria's coresponsibility for unleashing the First World War and to the folly of having gone to war against England.
4. See, however, the verses prefacing the novel, quoted below.
5. Perhaps the title may also imply that the novel is a ramp leading up to Doderer's *Die Dämonen*, then a "work in progress," which appeared in 1956 (Munich: Biederstein). See the publisher's note after p. 909.
6. Like the author, Stangeler has been a prisoner in Siberia: he is also a character in the novel *Das Geheimnis des Reiches* ("The Secret of the Empire," 1930), which deals with the life of captured Austrian soldiers there. He is well versed in the history of Vienna, and has studied at the University. (Doderer's excellent Vienna dissertation, written in 1925, deals with Austrian historiography in the fifteenth century. The similarity

between the dactylic names Stangeler and Doderer is also pertinent.

7. Doderer, *Grundlagen und Funktion des Romans* (Nuremberg: Glock and Lutz, 1959), p. 36.

8. Cf. Rilke's phrase "O hoher Baum im Ohr" in the *Sonette an Orpheus.*

9. "Un Romancier autrichien de la décadence," p. 528. For a sound, brief review of *Die Strudlhofstiege,* see Walter Grossmann in *Books Abroad,* XXVI (1952), 353–354.

10. Franz Lennartz, *Die Dichter unserer Zeit* (Stuttgart: Kröner, 1952), p. 90.

11. E. E. Noth, "Heimito von Doderer," *Cahiers du Sud,* LI (1964), 188.

12. *Grundlagen und Funktionen des Romans,* p. 40.

13. "Heimito von Doderer," p. 195.

14. "Gedanken zum Tod Heimito von Doderers," *Wort und Wahrheit,* XXII (1967), 154.

15. In conversation, Doderer remarked to me that Tyrolean "hillbillies" were notable for *foetor alpinus.*

16. See M. W. Swales, "The Narrator in the Novels of Heimito von Doderer" *Modern Language Review,* LXI (1966), 85–95, esp. p. 86.

17. *Die Wasserfälle von Slunj* (Munich: Biederstein, 1963), p. 45. References in the text are to this edition. Translations are my own.

18. See Hans Kricheldorff, "Heimito von Doderer: Roman No. 7," *Neue Deutsche Hefte,* No. 97 (Feb., 1964), p. 137.

19. See Swales, "The Narrator in the Novels of Heimito von Doderer."

20. Kricheldorff, "Heimito von Doderer," p. 137.

21. *The Future of the Novel* (New York: Vintage Books, 1956), p. 232.

22. Kricheldorff, "Heimito von Doderer," p. 136.

23. *Die Wasserfälle von Slunj,* p. 311.

Chapter 7. Squaring the Circle: Hermann Broch's *The Sleepwalkers*

1. "Jenseits von Joyce und Kafka," *Neue Rundschau*, LXIII (1952), 153–159.
2. Cf. Karl R. Mandelkow, *Hermann Brochs Romantrilogie "Die Schlafwandler"* (Heidelberg: Winter, 1962), pp. 35–56.
3. See Leo Kreutzer, *Erkenntnistheorie und Prophetie*, on *The Sleepwalkers* (Tübingen: Niemeyer, 1966), p. 194.
4. Hermann Broch, *Gesammelte Werke* (Zurich: Rhein-Verlag, 1953–1961), II, 400 (cited hereafter as *Ges. W.*). Translations are my own.
5. Kreutzer, *Erkenntnistheorie und Prophetie*, p. 45.
6. See Broch's well-known essay "James Joyce und die Gegenwart," *Ges. W.*, VI, 183–210.
7. See Kreutzer's analysis of Broch's commentaries, in *Erkenntnistheorie und Prophetie*, pp. 15–18, 26.
8. See *ibid.*, esp. p. 104.
9. *Ges. W.*, VI, 185–186.
10. *Ibid.*, pp. 191–193.
11. Cf. *ibid.*, VIII, 26, and Theodore Ziolkowski, *Hermann Broch* (New York and London: Columbia University Press, 1964), p. 16.
12. Acts 16:28.
13. P. 160. Page numbers in the text refer to *Die Schlafwandler* as printed in *Ges. W.*, II.
14. See Thomas Koebner, *Hermann Broch* (Bern: Francke, 1965), p. 26.
15. See Frank Trommler, *Roman und Wirklichkeit* (Stuttgart: Kohlhammer, 1966), p. 109.
16. Robert Musil, *Der Mann ohne Eigenschaften* (Hamburg: Rowohlt, 1952), p. 55.
17. *Ges. W.*, VIII, 18.
18. *Ibid.*, 104.

19. Cf. Koebner, *Hermann Broch*, p. 23.

20. *Ges. W.*, VIII, 26, 18.

21. A phrase used to describe another essentially religious person, Pharaoh Ikhnaton in *Joseph in Egypt.*

22. *Ges. W.*, VIII, 19.

23. *Ibid.*, II, 324. Cf. Mandelkow, *Hermann Brochs Romantrilogie*, p. 129.

24. Kreutzer, *Erkenntnistheorie und Prophetie*, p. 146.

25. *Ges. W.*, VIII, 26.

26. *Ibid.*, p. 19.

27. Bertrand Müller is not Eduard von Bertrand, as has been conjectured; he resembles him but is much more the ethical man.

28. *James Joyce* (Norfolk, Conn.: New Directions, 1960), p. 207.

29. *Ges. W.*, VIII, 19.

30. The murder is not based on sexual jealousy. Although Huguenau loathes Esch, his crime seems to be basically a "gratuitous act."

31. *Ges. W.*, VIII, 26.

32. In Broch's letter to Friedrich Torberg of April 10, 1943, Hitler is defined as "an instrument of the new age," As such, although completely evil, he has played his dialectical part (*Ges. W.*, VIII, 188).

33. J. W. von Goethe, *Werke* (Hamburg: Wegner), XII (1958), 470 (my translation).

34. Broch criticized Gide for "using a novel as a frame for psychoanalytical and other learned excursuses" (*Ges. W.*, VIII, 195–196). In her introduction to this volume, Hannah Arendt surmises that Broch was indirectly criticizing *The Sleepwalkers* (p. 11).

35. *Tagebücher, Aphorismen Essays und Reden* (Hamburg: Rowohlt, 1955), p. 567.

36. *Ges. W.*, VIII, 162.

37. *Doktor Faustus* (Frankfort on the Main and Berlin, 1948), p. 776.

38. According to this technique, every incident or other detail on one level must exactly correspond to its analogues on all other levels. Thus Leverkühn's career is parallel to the course of German politics, to the events of the Faust legend, and so on. (See Chapter 10 of this book.)

39. *Ges. W.*, VI, 208.

40. *Ibid.*, V, 360, 365. Broch's argument at this point is essentially the same as Schiller's in his *Briefe über die ästhetische Erziehung*.

41. *Ges. W.*, VI, 206–207.

Chapter 8. The Artist as Satirist: Günter Grass

1. *Ausgefragt* (Neuwied and Berlin: Luchterhand, 1967), p. 91. I thank Hermann Luchterhand Verlag GMBH for permission to quote from "Kleckerburg" and "Nächtliches Stadion."

2. Quoted by Kurt Lothar Tank, *Günter Grass* (Berlin: Luchterhand, 1965), p. 15.

3. Albert Soergel and Curt Hohoff, *Dichtung und Dichter der Zeit* (Düsseldorf: Bagel, 1961–1963), II, 826.

4. *Handwörterbuch des deutschen Aberglaubens* (Berlin and Leipzig: de Gruyter, 1924–1942).

5. Günter Grass, *The Tin Drum*, trans. Ralph Manheim (New York: Pantheon Books, 1961), p. 64. Page references to this translation are included hereafter in the text.

6. Thomas Mann, *Gesammelte Werke* (Frankfort on the Main: S. Fischer, 1960), X, 21.

7. "Aspects of Myth, Parody, and Obscenity in Günter Grass's *Die Blechtrommel* and *Katz und Maus*," *Germanic Review*, XL (1965), 240–250.

8. "The Grotesque Everyman in Günter Grass's *Die Blechtrommel*," *Monatshefte*, LVIII (1966), 131–138.

9. See Tank, *Günter Grass*, p. 77.

10. From "Inschrift auf einem sächsisch-preussischen Grenzstein," in Erich Kästner, *Gesang zwischen den Stühlen* (Stuttgart: Deutsche Verlags-Anstalt, 1932), p. 37 (all rights reserved by the publishing house of Kiepenheuer & Witsch).

11. *Dog Years*, trans. Ralph Manheim (New York: Harcourt, Brace, and World, 1965), p. 377. Page references are to this edition.

12. The passage was translated by me, since the corresponding passage in *Dog Years* has been much altered from the original text.

Chapter 9. A World Divided: Uwe Johnson's *Two Views*

1. See Johnson's "Eine Reise wegwohin, 1960," in his *Karsch und andere Prosa* (Frankfort on the Main: Suhrkamp, 1964), pp. 29–81.

2. See Horst Bienek, *Werkstattsgespräche mit Schriftstellern* (Munich: Hanser, 1962), p. 96.

3. Marcel Reich-Ranicki seems correct in inferring a strong resistance to "socialist realism" in these novels. See *Deutsche Literatur in West und Ost* (Munich: Pieper, 1963), p. 236.

4. Günter Blöcker, *Literatur als Teilhabe* (Berlin: Argon, 1966), pp. 35, 37.

5. W. M. Guggenheimer, in Johnson's *Karsch und andere Prosa*, p. 88.

6. See Harry Levin, *James Joyce* (rev. ed.; Norfolk, Conn.: New Directions, 1960), p. 220.

7. *Karsch und andere Prosa*, p. 60.

8. See *Evergreen Review*, V (1961), 18–34.

9. "Berliner Stadtbahn," *Merkur*, XV (1961), 725.

10. *Ibid.*, p. 727.

11. Blöcker, *Literatur als Teilhabe*, p. 34.

12. P. 239. Page references in the text pertain to *Zwei Ansichten* (Frankfort on the Main: Suhrkamp, 1965). Translations are my own.

13. Hugo Steger points out in *Zwischen Sprache und Literatur* (Göttingen: Sachse and Pohl, 1967), p. 46, how naïve such comments are.

14. Herbert Kolb, "Rückfall in die Parataxe," *Neue Deutsche Hefte*, No. 96 (1963), p. 55.

15. Kolb does not use the word "relapse" in a derogatory sense.

16. Quoted by Kolb, "Rückfall in die Parataxe," p. 68, from Johnson, *Mutmassungen über Jakob* (Frankfort on the Main: Suhrkamp, 1959), p. 12.

17. *Zwischen Sprache und Literatur*, esp. p. 67.

18. See H. G. Gräf, *Goethe über seine Dichtungen*, Part I, vol. I (Frankfort on the Main: Rutten and Loening, 1901), 487.

Chapter 10. The Magic Square: Thomas Mann's *Doctor Faustus*

1. "Thomas Mann's *Doctor Faustus:* The Enigma of Frau von Tolna," *Germanic Review*, XXIII (1948), 249–253; "Full Fathom Five: Notes on Some Devices in Thomas Mann's *Doctor Faustus*," *ibid.*, XXIV (1949), 274–278; "Thomas Mann and the Mermaid: A Note on Constructivistic Music," *Modern Language Notes, LXV* (1950), 171–175.

2. *Thomas Manns Doktor Faustus* (Stockholm: Svenska Bokförlaget, 1963).

3. Fru Bergsten made extensive use of the Thomas Mann Archive in Zurich, the best collection of works by and on Mann.

4. "Die gesellschaftliche Bedeutung der Musik im Werk von Thomas Mann," *Wissenschaftliche Zeitschrift der . . . Universität Jena*, III (1953–1954), Nos. 2–3.

5. Bergsten, *Thomas Manns Doktor Faustus*, p. 226.

6. "A Modern Faust," *Orbis Litterarum*, XX (1960), 176–204.

7. "The Vision of Doktor Faustus," *Germanic Review*, XL (1965), 277–309.

8. There is indeed a mathematical scheme in the arrangement of the forty-nine chapters, but it seems to be of relatively minor importance, though it is interesting that chapter xxv, the dialogue with the Devil, stands exactly in the center, and that chapter xxxiv, a particularly important unit, bears a "magic number" familiar from *The Magic Mountain.*

9. See also Mann's account of his debt to Theodor Adorno and others for musical information in *Die Entstehung des Doktor Faustus* (Amsterdam: S. Fischer, 1949); J. M. Stein's "Adrian Leverkühn as a Composer," *Germanic Review*, XXV (1950), 257–274; and Bodo Heimann, "Thomas Manns *Doktor Faustus* und die Musikphilosophie Adornos," *Deutsche Vierteljahresschrift*, XXXVIII (1964), 248–266.

10. The text used is Thomas Mann, *Doktor Faustus* (Stockholm: Bermann-Fischer Verlag, 1947). Translations are my own.

11. See Joachim Müller, "Thomas Manns *Doktor Faustus:* Grundthema und Motivgefüge," *Euphorion*, LIV (1960), 276.

12. William H. Rey, "Return to Health?: 'Disease' in Mann's *Doctor Faustus*," *PMLA*, LXV (1950), 21–26.

13. J. Elema, "Thomas Mann, Dürer und Doktor Faustus," *Euphorion*, LIX (1965), 97–117; also Walther Rehm, *Späte Studien* (Bern and Munich: Francke, 1964), pp. 344–358.

14. Edward Engelberg, "Thomas Mann's Faust and Beethoven," *Monatshefte*, XLVII (1955), 112–116.

15. The order in which the themes and levels are listed here is of no significance.

16. See Heimann's "Thomas Manns *Doktor Faustus* und die Musikphilosophie Adornos."

17. See J. M. Stein, "Adrian Leverkühn as a Composer."

18. "Full Fathom Five," p. 175. (See n. 1, above.)

19. Mann wrote of the secret identity of Zeitblom and Leverkühn. See *Gesammelte Werke* (Frankfort on the Main: S. Fischer, 1960), XI, 204.

20. Thomas Mann, *Briefe, 1889–1936*, ed. Erika Mann (Frankfort on the Main: S. Fischer, 1961), pp. 45, 52.

21. *Die Entstehung des Doktor Faustus*, p. 165.

22. "Adrian Leverkühns Leben als bewusste mythologische imitatio des Doktor Faustus," *Orbis Litterarum*, XX (1965), 128–158.

23. Adrian does not consciously "imitate" Nietzsche; the philosopher's name is not mentioned in the book, for the obvious reason that he "is" Leverkühn.

24. Bergsten, *Thomas Manns Doktor Faustus*, pp. 211–258.

25. P. 273. Fru Bergsten applies this insight directly to "The Lamentation of Doctor Faustus." Heimann argues that Mann did not dare to "break through" in the novel, since it is not primitive, elemental, or barbaric ("Thomas Manns *Doktor Faustus* und die Musikphilosophie Adornos," p. 265). But despite the devil's arguments, Mann showed that one can break through *without* selling one's soul.

SELECTIVE BIBLIOGRAPHY

This list is intended for the general reader and is focused on works in English.

Modern Fiction

Bithell, Jethro. *Modern German Literature, 1880–1950.* 3d ed. London: Methuen, 1959.

Freedman, Ralph. *The Lyrical Novel.* Princeton: Princeton University Press, 1963.

Hatfield, Henry. *Modern German Literature.* New York: St. Martin's Press, 1967; and Bloomington, Ind.: Indiana University Press, 1968 (paperback).

Jens, Walter. *Statt einer Literaturgeschichte.* 2d ed. Pfullingen: Neske, 1958.

Lange, Victor. *Modern German Literature.* Ithaca, N.Y.: Cornell University Press, 1945.

Lubbock, Percy. *The Craft of Fiction.* London: Cape, 1963.

Muir, Edwin. *The Structure of the Novel.* London: Hogarth, 1963.

Pascal, Roy. *The German Novel: Studies.* Toronto: University of Toronto Press, 1956.

Reich-Ranicki, Marcel. *Deutsche Literatur in West und Ost.* Munich: Piper, 1966.

Soergel, Albert, and Curt Hohoff. *Dichtung und Dichter der Zeit.* 2 vols. Düsseldorf: Bagel, 1961–1963.

Stern, J. P. *Reinterpretations.* London: Thames and Hudson, 1964.

Waidson, H. M. *The Modern German Novel.* London: Oxford University Press, 1960.

Individual Authors

Books Abroad, XLII (1968), No. 3 (Doderer issue).

Brinkmann, Richard. *Theodor Fontane*. Munich: Piper, 1967.

Demetz, Peter. *Formen des Realismus: Theodor Fontane*. Munich: Hanser, 1964.

Durzak, Manfred. *Herman Broch: Der Dichter und seine Zeit*. Stuttgart: Kohlhammer, 1968.

Emrich, Wilhelm. *Franz Kafka*. Bonn: Athenäum, 1961.

Hatfield, Henry. *Thomas Mann*. Rev. ed. Norfolk, Conn.: New Directions, 1962.

Hayens, Kenneth. *Theodor Fontane*. London: W. Collins, 1920.

Heller, Erich. *The Ironic German: A Study of Thomas Mann*. Boston and Toronto: Little, Brown, 1958.

Pike, Burton. *Robert Musil: An Introduction to His Work*. Ithaca, N.Y.: Cornell University Press, 1961.

Politzer, Heinz. *Franz Kafka: Parable and Paradox*. Ithaca, N.Y.: Cornell University Press, 1966.

Rose, Ernst. *Faith from the Abyss: Hermann Hesse's Way from Romanticism to Modernity*. New York: New York University Press, 1965.

Sokel, Walter. *Franz Kafka: Tragik und Ironie*. Munich: Langenmüller, 1964.

Tank, Karl Lothar. *Günter Grass*. Berlin: Luchterhand, 1965.

Ziolkowski, Theodore. *Hermann Broch*. New York: Columbia University Press, 1964.

——. *The Novels of Hermann Hesse*. Princeton: Princeton University Press, 1965.

INDEX

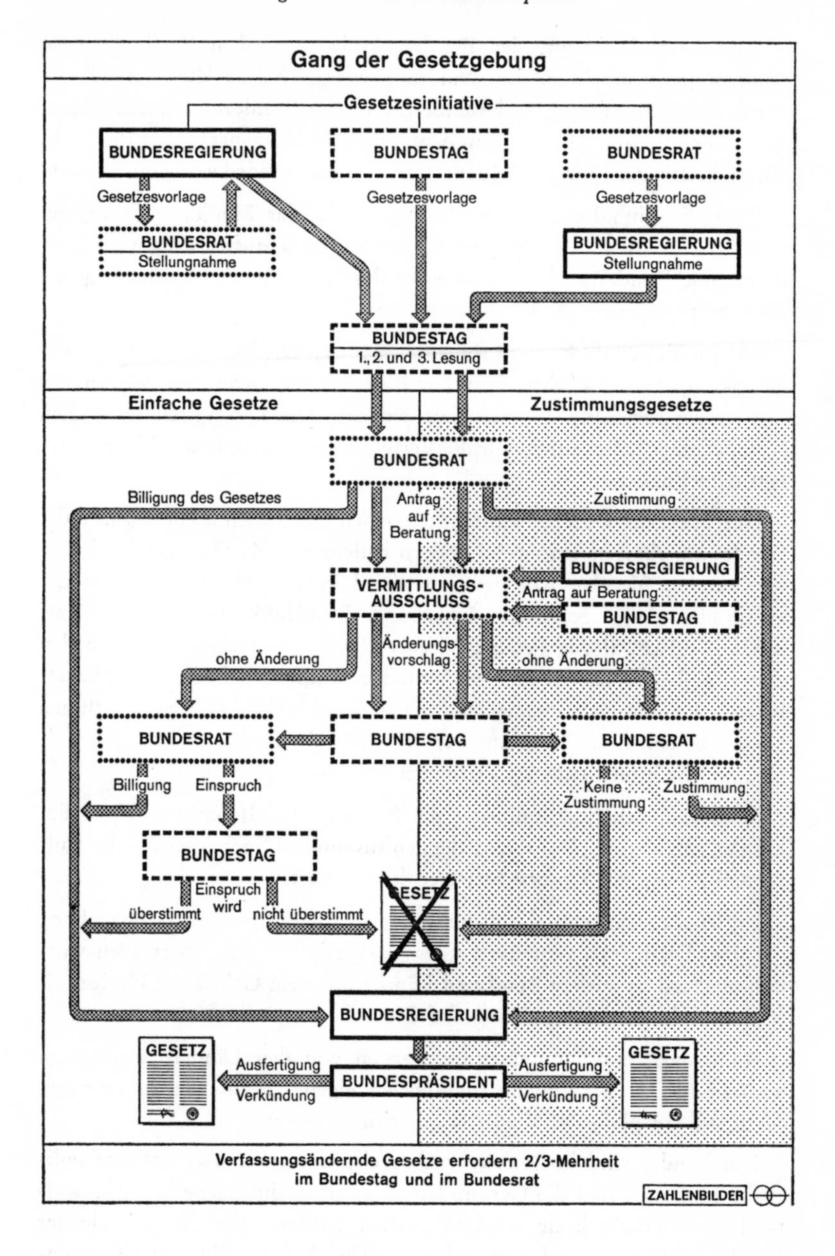
Gang der Gesetzgebung
Gesetzesinitiative
BUNDESREGIERUNG
BUNDESTAG
BUNDESRAT
Gesetzesvorlage
Gesetzesvorlage
Gesetzesvorlage
BUNDESRAT
Stellungnahme
BUNDESREGIERUNG
Stellungnahme
BUNDESTAG
1., 2. und 3. Lesung
Einfache Gesetze
Zustimmungsgesetze
BUNDESRAT
Billigung des Gesetzes
Antrag auf Beratung
Zustimmung
BUNDESREGIERUNG
VERMITTLUNGS-AUSSCHUSS
Antrag auf Beratung
BUNDESTAG
ohne Änderung
Änderungs-vorschlag
ohne Änderung
BUNDESRAT
BUNDESTAG
BUNDESRAT
Billigung
Einspruch
Keine Zustimmung
Zustimmung
BUNDESTAG
Einspruch wird
überstimmt
nicht überstimmt
GESETZ
BUNDESREGIERUNG
GESETZ
Ausfertigung
Verkündung
BUNDESPRÄSIDENT
Ausfertigung
Verkündung
GESETZ
Verfassungsändernde Gesetze erfordern 2/3-Mehrheit
im Bundestag und im Bundesrat
ZAHLENBILDER

Das Staatsoberhaupt, der Bundespräsident, wird nicht direkt vom Volk, sondern mit Hilfe von Wahlmännern gewählt. Diese Wahlmänner werden von Bundestag und Bundesrat in die Bundesversammlung entsandt, die alle fünf Jahre nur zu dem Zweck zusammentritt, den Präsidenten zu bestimmen. Jeder Präsident darf nur einmal wiedergewählt werden.

Über die Einhaltung der Verfassung wacht das Bundesverfassungsgericht in Karlsruhe. Das Verfassungsgericht kann auf Antrag von Bundestag und Bundesrat dem Präsidenten das Amt entziehen, wenn er gegen die Verfassung und die Gesetze verstößt.

Die Bundesrepublik ist ein föderativer Staat. Die Verteilung der Regierungskompetenz zwischen Bund und Ländern ist von den Vätern der Verfassung sorgfältig ausbalanciert worden. Die wichtigsten staatlichen Kompetenzen, wie Außenpolitik, Verteidigung, Recht und Währung stehen dem Bund zu.

Um aber ein Gegengewicht gegen einen möglichen Zentralismus des Bundes zu schaffen, sind den Ländern bedeutende Zuständigkeiten belassen worden. Zu den Kompetenzen der Länder gehören vor allem die kulturellen Angelegenheiten, Erziehung, Rundfunk, Fernsehen, Polizei sowie die Verwaltung gewisser Steuern. Auf den Gebieten, die zu den Zuständigkeiten der Länder gehören, verständigen sich die Fachminister regelmäßig, um gemeinsame im ganzen Bundesgebiet gültige Richtlinien auszuarbeiten. Eine Auseinanderentwicklung des Rechts und der Verwaltungspraxis in den einzelnen Ländern wird so vermieden.

Es gibt keinen Kultusminister des Bundes. Die elf Kultusminister der Länder haben eine „Konferenz der Kultusminister“ gebildet, die die Kulturpolitik und das Unterrichtswesen koordiniert.

Inzwischen ist durch Verfassungsänderung dem Bund die Gesetzgebung für die allgemeinen Grundsätze des Universitätswesens übertragen worden. Außerdem wirken Bund und Länder auf dem Gebiet des Hochschulbaus und der Bildungsplanung und Forschung zusammen.

Rundfunk- und Fernsehsender werden von den Ländern gemeinsam verwaltet. Der Versuch des Bundes, ein eigenes Fernsehen zu gründen, scheiterte am Nein des Verfassungsgerichtes.

Die Länder sind in Bezirke und Kreise unterteilt. Als unterste politische Einheiten sind die Gemeinden zu nennen, die eigene Selbstverwaltung besitzen. Auch sie erhalten gewisse Steuern, die sie nach eigener Wahl zum Gemeinwohl verwenden können. Auf der Ebene der Gemein-